ICE CREAM SANDWICHES

Ice Cream Sandwiches

65 RECIPES for INCREDIBLY COOL TREATS

DONNA EGAN

TEN SPEED PRESS
Berkeley

FOR MY DAUGHTERS, AUDREY AND AMELIA:
OFTEN PATIENT, USUALLY ENCOURAGING, ALWAYS INSPIRING.

Originally published in Great Britain by Ebury Press, an imprint of Ebury Publishing,
the Random House Group Ltd., London, in 2012

Library of Congress Cataloging-in-Publication Data is on file with the publisher

Hardcover ISBN 978-1-60774-495-5
eBook ISBN 978-1-60774-496-2

Printed in China

Design by Friederike Huber and Katy Brown
Photography by William Reavell
Food styling by Denise Smart
Prop styling by Jessica Georgiades

10 9 8 7 6 5 4 3 2 1

First American Edition

CONTENTS

INTRODUCTION

Cool, creamy vanilla ice cream surrounded by crunchy, buttery oatmeal cookies. Chewy chocolaty brownies encasing refreshing mint–chocolate chip ice cream, indulgently dipped in slightly bitter chocolate. Ice cream sandwiches are among the sweetest memories of my childhood . . . just as much a part of summers growing up in California as running through the garden sprinklers in our swimsuits.

Ice cream sandwiches are traditionally made by sandwiching ice cream between two baked cookies or wafers. Combining the crunchy, chewy cookies with creamy, cold ice cream somehow more than doubles the resulting pleasure.

No wonder ice cream sandwiches have been a favorite treat for children and adults alike in the United States for generations. They made their debut in New York City in the 1890s and quickly caught on across the country with one particular version being honored as the Official Food of San Francisco. They eventually found their way to places as diverse as Australia, Scotland, and Singapore, where they are usually made by slipping a scoop of ice cream between two layers of rainbow-colored bread!

I launched my Buttercup Cake Shop in London in 2006. As we expanded into a premier cupcake company with locations in Kent and London (including the 2012 Olympics site), we started to get quite a few inquiries about whether we also sold ice cream. This got me thinking: what goes better with cake than ice cream? We began offering cupcakes blended with vanilla ice cream and called it a cupshake, ice cream on top of cupcakes (cupcake sundaes), and my childhood favorite, ice cream sandwiches.

Ice cream sandwiches made their UK debut at Buttercup in spring 2011 and proved instantly popular. We bake the cookies fresh every day and assemble the sandwiches to order on the spot, so they are soft and ready to enjoy immediately. Although initially I envisioned them being mostly popular with children, it turns out I wasn't the only adult keen to indulge! I especially get a kick out of watching stylish men in their twenties and thirties tuck in unreservedly. Today, ice cream sandwiches have become hotter than ever! They are the latest comfort food to receive gourmet status at bakeries and gelato shops in New York City, where endless combinations of ice cream and "cookie" are available.

In this book you will discover easy, step-by-step instructions on how to prepare, assemble, and decorate delicious and novel sandwiches. Rose Meringues (page 41) are ideal for a dinner party, and White Chocolate Chip Teddies (page 51) will be a hit at any child's birthday. In addition, try the special treats for seasonal celebrations, such as Graveyard Coffins (page 77) for Halloween and Flocked Trees (page 68) for Christmas. And when nothing but the most indulgent treat will suffice, try the Caramel Snickerdoodle-doos (page 12), an irresistible combination of vanilla, caramel, and cinnamon, or Aloha Sandwiches (page 16), a marriage of chocolate, toasted coconut, and macadamia nut that will transport you to paradise!

Whatever the occasion, you'll find that making ice cream sandwiches is straightforward. It's an activity that can be shared with children, and with some adult help, cutting and filling the sandwiches is not only easy but also boosts their confidence in the kitchen.

For ease of use, the recipes are divided into three sections: several chapters of sandwiches (with assembly and decoration ideas), the cookie recipes, and the main ice cream recipes. I have included recipes for ice cream you can make at home, including some that don't require an ice cream maker and still result in a creamy, smooth texture. The division of cookie and ice cream recipes also makes mixing and matching easier should you want to customize. Feel free to experiment with flavor combinations, add your own decorations, and adjust the portion sizes as you wish.

If you are short on time, there is always the option of using store-bought cookies and/or ice cream. You can easily make any of the cookies or ice creams a day ahead and do the assembly and decoration separately. Ice cream sandwiches can be stored in the freezer for several weeks, so they're perfect for impromptu get-togethers with friends, last-minute playdates, or when you crave a guilty pleasure.

I hope you will have fun in the kitchen with the recipes that follow and wish you pleasurable satisfaction with the resulting creations. Happy sandwiching!

COOKS' NOTES

EQUIPMENT

For all recipes requiring an ice cream maker, I use a simple 2-pint (1-liter) capacity model, where the bowl portion is popped into the freezer for at least several hours before adding ingredients and churning. With this type of machine, remember that the base must be fully refrozen between batches.

Specialty ice cream sandwich molds by Tovolo can be used for creating shapes and assembling, including making an imprint on the top of the sandwich. Wilton now sells a pour- or scoop-in sandwich mold that can be used for round brownie or cookie bases. Otherwise, standard cookie cutters may be used.

Baking times vary with different oven and pan types. For the brownies and bars, I use jelly-roll pans that measure about 15 by 10 by 1 inch (38 by 25 by 2.5 cm). For the cookie recipes, I use insulated cookie sheets. The recipes give conventional oven temperatures. However, I use a convection oven, which requires a lower oven temperature and often shorter cooking times. In many recipes, a range of cooking times is given to allow for potential adjustments.

INGREDIENTS

Throughout the book, for convenience I have given two sets of measures, standard US measures and metric. The latter is found in brackets. Always stick to one system throughout a recipe; never mix the two. "Cups" refer to the standard measuring cup, and for flour I have used the dip-and-sweep method of filling the cup, giving a generous measure. Metric weight measures have been rounded for convenience.

I've used extra-large eggs in nearly all cases, and the butter is unsalted. Creams vary by recipe. Using heavy cream will yield thicker, more decadent results than whipping cream, which produces an airier ice cream.

DECADENT

Whether it's toasted nuts, creamy caramel, chocolate mousse, or several of these combined, sometimes nothing but the most wickedly indulgent treat will do. When you have one of those occasions, this is the chapter for you! Here you can choose from options such as Chocolate Hazelnut Sandwiches (page 25), a light but rich combination of brownie, fluffy chocolate, and hazelnuts; Butter-scotchies (page 21), a sweet punch of chewy butterscotch brownie with custardy vanilla ice cream and home-made butterscotch sauce; and Caramel Snickerdoodle-doos (page 12), an innocent-enough name for a heady combination of cinnamon, vanilla, and caramel.

CARAMEL SNICKERDOODLE-DOOS

My mother would often treat us kids to a Saturday trip to the beach, and we always pestered her on the way home to stop by Marianne's, famous for its fifty-plus flavors of homemade ice cream. To this day, cinnamon caramel ice cream remains one of my favorites in the world. The same flavor combination is probably what makes this recipe so comforting and irresistible. Reassuringly, Marianne's can still be found in its original spot on Ocean Street in Santa Cruz, California, but for those too far away, give this recipe a try!

Makes 6 sandwiches

Butterscotch Sauce
⅓ cup (110 g) light corn syrup
½ cup plus 2 tablespoons (135 g) firmly packed light brown sugar
2 tablespoons (30 g) butter
⅛ teaspoon salt (about 3 pinches)
⅓ cup (80 ml) heavy cream

12 Snickerdoodle Cookies (page 85)
Vanilla Ice Cream (page 112), or 1 pint (480 ml) premium store-bought

1. To make the sauce, put the syrup, sugar, butter, and salt in a heavy saucepan and stir over medium heat. Bring to a boil and keep stirring until the mixture is the consistency of a thick syrup, then remove from the heat. Allow to cool for 10 minutes, then mix in the cream.
2. Make the ice cream as directed and remove the canister from the ice cream maker. Drizzle the butterscotch sauce over the soft ice cream and use a rubber spatula to marble it through before transferring to an airtight plastic storage container. (If using store-bought ice cream, take it out of the freezer to soften for 3 to 4 minutes before marbling with the butterscotch.) Freeze for at least 1 hour.
3. Make the cookies as directed and match similar sizes to make up pairs. Scoop your desired amount of ice cream onto the center of the flat side of 1 cookie. Using an offset spatula, spread it evenly to within ½ inch (1 cm) of 1 cookie edge. Place the matching cookie on top, flat side down, and gently press to spread the ice cream evenly to the edges. Repeat with the remaining cookies.
4. Serve immediately, or place in an airtight plastic container and put in the freezer. The sandwiches may be stacked, but the edges must not touch. If frozen, allow to sit at room temperature for about 3 minutes before enjoying.

PEANUT BUTTER DREAM

Those who like peanut butter won't be able to resist this combination of chocolate brownies sandwiched with fluffy peanut butter filling, adapted from a beloved recipe for peanut butter pie. This filling lends itself well to being sandwiched before freezing, and the sandwiches have the added benefit of holding their shape without melting.

Makes 6 sandwiches

12 Chewy Chocolate Brownies (page 82)
½ cup plus 1 tablespoon (140 ml) whipping cream
4 ounces (115 g) cream cheese
½ cup (130 g) smooth peanut butter
½ cup (100 g) granulated white sugar
2 teaspoons (10 g) butter, at room temperature
1 teaspoon pure vanilla extract

1. Bake the brownie base as directed, remembering to cut it as soon as it's out of the oven. Meanwhile, whip the cream in a small bowl until fluffy and set aside in the refrigerator or another cool place.
2. In a separate bowl, beat together the cream cheese, peanut butter, sugar, butter, and vanilla until smooth. Fold the whipped cream into the peanut butter mixture until no streaks remain.
3. Once the brownies are completely cool, arrange half of them bottom side up. Spread the desired amount of filling onto the bottom of 1 brownie, spreading it within about ¼ inch (5 mm) of the edges. Top with a second brownie, bottom side down, and press gently to spread the filling evenly to the edges. Repeat with the rest of the brownies.
4. Place in airtight plastic containers and freeze for at least 2 hours before serving.

ALOHA SANDWICHES

This recipe is inspired by many summers enjoyed in the Hawaiian sun on the island of Maui, where, among other treats, you'll find hula pie, a concoction of coffee and chocolate ice cream over a chocolate crumb base, smothered in fudge sauce and macadamia nuts.

Makes 4 large or 8 small sandwiches

All-American Chocolate Chip Cookie dough (page 88)
½ cup (40 g) shredded dried coconut, toasted
½ cup (60 g) macadamia nuts, lightly toasted and chopped
Chocolate or Mocha Ice Cream (page 112 or 114), or 1 pint (480 ml)
    store-bought, semisoftened

1. Bake the cookies as directed. While still warm from the oven, cut into 8 large or 16 small rectangles. (To make triangles, cut the large rectangles in half diagonally.) Allow to cool for at least 10 minutes before removing from the pan.
2. Spread the coconut on a flat plate and the chopped nuts on another plate. Once the cookies are completely cool, turn half of the cookies bottom side up. Spoon some semisoftened ice cream onto the center of the bottom of 1 cookie. Using an offset spatula, spread it evenly to within ¼ inch (5 mm) of the edges. Top with a second cookie, bottom side down, and press gently to spread the ice cream evenly to the edges. Add the second cookie, flat side down. Gently and evenly press together until the ice cream spreads to the edges.
3. Working quickly, press the edges of the sandwich in the coconut, then in the chopped nuts. Repeat with the rest of the cookies.
4. Serve immediately, or quickly store in a single layer in an airtight plastic container and freeze. If frozen, allow to sit for 3 minutes before serving.

BEVERLY HILLS DAHLINGS

Just like their namesake, these sandwiches manage to pay homage to healthy eating (thanks to the oatmeal) while being plenty rich and sporting their share of nuts! This recipe is best with homemade vanilla ice cream, but if you choose to substitute a store-bought ice cream, check the ingredients to ensure it's real dairy ice cream, rather than an inferior product made from whey protein and vegetable oils.

Makes 9 sandwiches

18 Beverly Hills Cookies (page 98)
Vanilla Ice Cream (page 112), or 1 pint (480 ml) premium store-bought
¾ cup (90 g) walnuts (optional), toasted and finely chopped

1. Make the cookies as directed and match up similar sizes to make pairs.
2. Working with ice cream that has fully set in the freezer (that is, not directly out of the ice cream maker, when it will be too messy), scoop your desired amount of ice cream onto the center of the flat side of 1 cookie. Using an offset spatula, spread it evenly to within ¼ inch (5 mm) of the edges. Sprinkle with the chopped walnuts.
3. Place the matching cookie on top, flat side down, and press gently to spread the ice cream evenly to the edges. Repeat with the remaining cookies.
4. Serve immediately, or place in an airtight plastic container and freeze until a few minutes before serving. The sandwiches may be stacked, but the edges must not touch.

MONKEY SANDWICHES

Monkeys love bananas and nuts, and so do kids . . . especially when combined with vanilla ice cream sandwiched between two brownies!

Makes 4 large or 8 small sandwiches

Chewy Chocolate Brownies (page 82)
½ cup (65 g) roasted peanuts, chopped
Vanilla Ice Cream (page 112), or 1 pint (480 ml) premium store-bought, softened
2 bananas, peeled and sliced

1. Bake the brownie base as directed. While still warm from the oven, cut into 8 large or 16 small rectangles. Allow to cool for at least 10 minutes before removing from the pan.
2. Spread the chopped peanuts on a flat plate. Once the brownies are completely cool, turn half of the brownies bottom side up. Spoon some of the ice cream onto the center of the bottom of 1 brownie. Using an offset spatula, spread it evenly to within ¼ inch (5 mm) of the edges.
3. Arrange the banana slices in a single layer, then top with a second brownie, bottom side down. Gently press together to spread the ice cream to the edges. Working quickly, roll the edges of the sandwich in the nuts. Repeat with the rest of the brownies.
4. Serve immediately, or quickly store in a single layer in an airtight plastic container and freeze. If frozen, allow to sit for 3 minutes before serving.

BUTTERSCOTCHIES

This is for when you are in the mood for something chewy and sweet! You can make the butterscotch sauce ahead and store it in the refrigerator.

Makes 4 large or 6 medium sandwiches

Butterscotch Brownie dough (page 84)
Butterscotch Sauce (page 12)
Vanilla Ice Cream (page 112), or 1 pint (480 ml) premium store-bought

1. Due to the butterscotch sauce, it is best to assemble these right before serving. If you prefer to make them ahead, have ready a couple of airtight plastic containers, kept cold in the freezer.
2. Bake the brownie base as directed. While still warm from the oven, cut into shapes as desired, ensuring to make pairs of the same size. Allow to cool before removing from the pan. Match up the pairs.
3. Ensure the butterscotch sauce has cooled to room temperature before assembling the sandwiches, to avoid melting the ice cream. Working with ice cream that has fully set in the freezer (that is, not directly out of the ice cream maker, when it will be too messy), scoop your desired amount of ice cream onto the center of the bottom of 1 brownie. Using an offset spatula, spread it evenly to within ¼ inch (5 mm) of the edges.
4. Make a small well in the center of the ice cream and spoon 1 to 2 teaspoons of the butterscotch sauce into the well. Work with cooled sauce if possible; however, if it is proving too difficult to scoop, warm it up in the microwave for just 5 seconds or warm gently in a heatproof bowl set over a pan of hot (not boiling) water.
5. Place the matching brownie on top, bottom side down, and press gently to spread the ice cream evenly to the edges. Repeat with the remaining brownies.
6. Serve immediately if possible. Otherwise, pop the sandwiches into your cold plastic containers without stacking (to avoid the butterscotch running over the outside of the brownie) and put in the freezer. If frozen, let sit for 3 minutes before serving.

BOUNTY BITES

Somehow the pleasure of chewy coconut cookies and chocolate ice cream, when combined, is more than the sum of their parts. These will retain their maximum chewiness and flavor if you fill them just before serving.

Makes 8 medium or 16 bite-size sandwiches

16 medium or 32 bite-size Coconut Macaroons (page 96; note instruction
    below if adding cocoa)
2 tablespoons cocoa powder (optional)
Chocolate Ice Cream (page 112), or 1 pint (480 ml) premium store-bought

1. Make the macaroons as directed. If adding the cocoa in this recipe, first heat the sweetened condensed milk in a pan over low heat, then whisk in the 2 table-spoons cocoa powder until well combined. Remove from the heat and use as directed.
2. Once the macaroons have baked and cooled, match up similar sizes to make pairs. Scoop your desired amount of ice cream onto the flat side of the first macaroon. Use an offset spatula or dull knife to spread the ice cream to within ¼ inch (5 mm) of the edges.
3. Top with the second macaroon, flat side down, and gently press to spread the ice cream to the edges. Repeat with the remaining macaroons.
4. Serve immediately, or place in an airtight plastic container and put in the freezer. The sandwiches may be stacked, but the edges must not touch. If frozen, allow to sit at room temperature for about 3 minutes before serving.

CHOCOLATE HAZELNUT SANDWICHES

These are best made with my chocolate ice cream, which is made like a mousse and uses semisweet chocolate, so it has a more decadent, less sugary effect than commercial chocolate ice creams. You can toast the hazelnuts for extra flavor and can also opt to add coffee liqueur when entertaining adult friends. This sandwich also works well with Tin Roof Cookies (page 101) or Mocha Cookies (page 104).

Makes 6 to 8 sandwiches

Chocolate Ice Cream (page 112)
¼ cup (60 ml) coffee liqueur (optional)
⅓ cup (50 g) hazelnuts, chopped
Chewy Chocolate Brownies (page 82)

1. Make the base for the ice cream as directed, but when folding the chocolate into the whipped cream mixture, also fold in the coffee liqueur and hazelnuts in this recipe. Freeze as directed.
2. Meanwhile, bake the brownie base as directed. While still warm from the oven, cut into 12 to 16 desired shapes, remembering to cut shapes in pairs. If your cutter is not symmetrical, cut every other brownie with the opposite side of the cutter so that they will match up into sandwiches. Allow to cool before removing from the pan.
3. Scoop your desired amount of ice cream onto the center of the bottom of 1 brownie. Using an offset spatula, spread it evenly to within ½ inch (1 cm) of the edges. Place the matching brownie on top, bottom side down, and press gently to spread the ice cream evenly to the edges. Repeat with the remaining brownies.
4. Place the sandwiches in an airtight plastic container. If you need to stack them, place sheets of waxed paper between the layers. Freeze until ready to serve. Allow to sit at room temperature for 3 minutes before serving.

MOCHA MORSELS

This recipe, combining two of my favorite flavors—coffee and chocolate—is sure to please even your more sophisticated guests. For a richer flavor, you can sprinkle a layer of cocoa powder over the ice cream before adding the top cookie.

Makes 6 sandwiches

12 Mocha Cookies (page 104)
Mocha Ice Cream (page 114)

1. Make the cookies as directed and let cool. Make the ice cream as directed but don't freeze it after churning.
2. Once the cookies are fully cooled, match up similar sizes to make pairs. Using an offset spatula, spread a layer of ice cream ¾ inch (2 cm) thick onto the flat side of 1 cookie, smoothing the edges. Place the matching cookie, flat side down, on top. Repeat with the remaining cookies.
3. Carefully place the sandwiches in an airtight plastic container. If you need to stack them, place sheets of waxed paper between the layers. Freeze for at least 1½ hours before serving. Once frozen, allow to sit for 3 minutes before serving.

BANOFFEE SANDWICHES

The banoffee cupcakes at Buttercup are the favorite choice of our male customers, so that was the inspiration behind this recipe, which combines fresh banana bread with vanilla ice cream and butterscotch sauce.

Makes 6 sandwiches

Vanilla Ice Cream (page 112), or 1 pint (480 ml) premium store-bought
Butterscotch Sauce (page 12)
1 loaf or 6 mini loaves Banana Bread (page 106)
½ cup (120 ml) butterscotch or white chocolate curls or chips (optional)

1. Make the ice cream as directed and remove the canister from the ice cream maker. (If using store-bought, remove from the freezer to soften for 3 to 4 minutes only, or microwave on 80 percent power for 10 to 15 seconds.) Drizzle the butterscotch sauce over the soft ice cream, then use a rubber spatula to marble it through. Transfer to an airtight plastic container and freeze for at least 1 hour.
2. Use this time to make the Banana Bread as directed. Once cooled, cut the Banana Bread into slices a generous ½ inch (1.5 cm) thick. If you opted for the full-size loaf, cut each slice in half to form 2 rectangles. If you made mini loaves, slice each one in half horizontally.
3. Spread the butterscotch curls on a flat plate. Scoop your desired amount of ice cream into the center of the cut side of 1 slice. Using an offset spatula, spread it evenly to within ½ inch (1 cm) of the edges. Place the matching slice on top, cut side down, and press gently to spread the ice cream evenly to the edges. Press the edges of the sandwich in the butterscotch curls. Repeat with the remaining slices.
4. These should ideally be served immediately. If you cannot serve right away, place in an airtight plastic container (the sandwiches can be stacked) and return to the freezer. If frozen, allow to sit for a couple of minutes at room temperature before serving.

GINGER LEMON GEMS

Ginger lovers will especially appreciate its pairing with my zesty lemon ice cream. The intense flavors make these smaller-size gems a perfect accompaniment to a light afternoon tea. When making the ice cream, ensure you use real dairy cream. Ultra-high-temperature cream will work, but avoid dairy substitutes, which are made mostly with oil.

Makes 12 small sandwiches

Soft Ginger Cookie dough (page 92)
Lemon Ice Cream (page 115)

1. Follow the recipe for the cookies and drop 24 balls of the mixture onto the cookie sheet from a spring-action melon baller (or arrange heaped teaspoons). Reduce the baking time to 4 to 6 minutes, then cool as directed.
2. Once the cookies have completely cooled, match up similar sizes to make pairs. Spoon some of the ice cream onto the flat side of 1 cookie and gently place the second cookie, flat side down, on top, pressing only enough to adhere to the ice cream. Repeat with the remaining cookies.
3. Place the sandwiches—without stacking—in an airtight plastic container and freeze for at least 1 hour. Take out of the freezer immediately before serving.

FRESH 'N' FRUITY

Although commercially available ice cream sandwiches nearly always include a combination of vanilla and chocolate, for some occasions you may prefer something lighter, fresh, and fruity. On the following pages you will find a plethora of options, including the very light Lemon Creams (page 38), Melon Sorbet Butterflies (page 42), and a creamy, custardy fresh fig ice cream spread between two Rolled Vanilla Cookies (page 34). One of my favorites here is the tangy Mascarpone Ice Cream sandwiched between soft and spicy Pumpkin Spice Cookies (page 46), the perfect finale to an autumn-themed meal.

APPLE PIE À LA MODE

A satisfying treat at any time of year but especially welcome in the autumn when apples are plentiful.

Makes 9 sandwiches

18 Grated Apple Cookies (page 91)
Vanilla Ice Cream (page 112), or 1 pint (480 ml) premium store-bought

1. Prepare the cookies as directed. Allow them to cool completely then match up similar sizes to make pairs.
2. Scoop the desired amount of ice cream onto the flat side of the first cookie. Use an offset spatula or dull knife to spread the ice cream to within ¼ inch (5 mm) of the edges. Top with the second cookie, flat side down, and press gently to spread the ice cream to the edges. Neaten up the sides with the spatula if desired. Repeat with the remaining cookies.
3. Serve immediately, or store in the freezer in an airtight plastic container. If frozen, allow to sit at room temperature for 3 minutes before serving.

PEACHES 'N' CREAM

Peaches epitomize summer and make an ice cream that is both refreshing and indulgent. When paired with a classic Rolled Vanilla Cookie, the result is sumptuous! You can substitute nectarines for peaches, but ensure either is perfectly ripe.

Makes 8 or more sandwiches

Rolled Vanilla Cookie dough (page 80)
4 egg yolks
¼ teaspoon salt
¾ cup (150 g) granulated white sugar
2 cups plus 6 tablespoons (570 ml) heavy cream
6 tablespoons (90 ml) milk
2½ cups (500 g) mashed peaches (7 or 8, depending on size)

1. Prepare and bake the cookie dough as directed, cutting into your desired shapes. If you are using a sandwich mold or cookie cutter with a pattern, use while the cookies are still hot from the oven, carefully pressing down on the mold or cutter to imprint the pattern onto half of the cookies. Cool completely, then match up similar sizes into pairs.
2. Beat the egg yolks in a blender or with an electric mixer until thick. Add the salt, then beat in the sugar in three batches. Scald 6 tablespoons (90 ml) of the cream with all the milk in a heatproof bowl over a pan of simmering water.
3. Stir a small amount of the milk mixture into the egg yolk mixture. Then add all the yolk mixture to the milk mixture and cook, stirring constantly over simmering water, until the mixture forms a custard thick enough to coat the back of the spoon. Remove from the heat and let cool.
4. Mix the mashed fruit with the remaining 2 cups (480 ml) of cream, stir in the custard mixture, and refrigerate until cold. Pour into an ice cream maker and follow the manufacturer's instructions. Freeze for at least 2 hours before using as a filling.
5. If you used a sandwich mold or tall cutter, refit the first cookie, bottom side up, in the base of the mold or under the cutter. Place the body of the mold over as a guide for adding ice cream and fill to your desired thickness. Remove the mold or cutter and gently place the top cookie, right side up, on top of the ice cream. Repeat with the remaining cookies.
6. Serve immediately, or place in an airtight plastic container and freeze. The sandwiches may be stacked, but the edges must not touch.

FRESH FIG (PIG) SANDWICHES

The combination of rich custard and fresh figs makes a delightful, indulgent filling, and combined with vanilla cookies, it makes a lovely end-of-summer treat.

Makes 12 sandwiches

Rolled Vanilla Cookie dough (page 80)
4 extra-large eggs
1 cup (200 g) granulated white sugar
2 cups (480 ml) milk
2 cups (480 ml) heavy or whipping cream
1½ teaspoons pure vanilla extract
¼ teaspoon salt
¼ teaspoon ground nutmeg
4 fresh figs, peeled and mashed

1. Make the cookie dough as directed. While the dough is chilling, make the ice cream as follows.
2. Beat the eggs in a blender until thick or use an electric mixer. Beat in the sugar in three batches. Combine with the milk and cream in a heatproof bowl, put over a pan of simmering, but not boiling, water (or in a double boiler) and cook, stirring constantly, until it becomes a thick custard.
3. Remove from the heat and stir in the vanilla extract, salt, and nutmeg. Fold in the mashed figs. Refrigerate until cool, then pour into an ice cream maker and follow the manufacturer's instructions. Freeze for at least 2 hours before filling.
4. Use this freezing time to bake the cookie dough. Use a shaped cutter or a knife to cut out 24 cookies. If you are making imprints on the top of your cookies, do this to half of them while they are still hot and before removing from the cookie sheet. Once the cookies are fully cooled, match them up into pairs.
5. If using a mold, place 1 cookie, bottom side up, in the mold. Add ice cream, using the mold to guide its shape. Push down gently with the plunger to distribute the ice cream evenly into shape. Remove the mold, then place a second cookie, bottom side down, on top of the ice cream.
6. If not using a mold, take an offset spatula and spread ice cream evenly to within ¼ inch (5 mm) of the edges. Place another cookie on top, bottom side down, and press gently until the ice cream spreads to the edges. Repeat with the remaining cookies. Serve immediately, or freeze in airtight plastic containers (they can be stacked). If frozen, allow to sit for 3 minutes before serving.

ELDERFLOWER AMARETTOS

Elderflower is a quintessentially English flavor that I only discovered once I'd lived in the United Kingdom for a few years. It's now one of my favorite flavors. My neighbor Catriona showed me how simple it is to make a syrup for cordials, and I found that it easily adjusted for this sorbet, too.

Pick elderflower heads that are growing away from the roadside, where they might be dusty, and reach for the higher limbs, as those are the cleanest. Find buds that are open but have not yet started to wilt. Ensure you are collecting elderflower and not a look-alike by checking against photos (available online), and, of course, use your nose to confirm the distinctive sweet scent.

Makes 6 to 8 sandwiches

3½ cups (700 g) superfine sugar
4½ cups (1 liter) water
Grated zest and juice of 2 lemons
10 elderflower heads
12 to 16 Amaretto Biscuits (page 99)

1. First make a sugar syrup by placing the sugar and water in a large saucepan over medium heat. Stir constantly until the sugar has dissolved. Then increase the heat just until the mixture boils. Lower the heat to maintain a steady simmer and cook until thickened (about 5 minutes).
2. Remove from the heat and stir in the lemon zest and elderflower heads. Cool, then strain to remove the flowers. Stir in the lemon juice and refrigerate until cold. While waiting, make the biscuits as directed.
3. Put the cold elderflower mixture into an ice cream maker and follow the manufacturer's instructions. Transfer to an airtight plastic container, allowing at least ½ inch (1 cm) of empty space at the top of the container. Allow to freeze for at least 1½ hours.
4. Make sure the biscuits are fully cooked, then match up similar-size biscuits to make pairs. Apply a scoop of sorbet to the middle of the flat side of 1 biscuit. Flatten with an offset spatula or dull knife. Then use the flat side of the matching biscuit to gently press down until the sorbet nearly spreads to the edges. Repeat with the remaining biscuits.
5. It's best to serve immediately, as these cookies can become brittle when frozen.

LEMON CREAMS

The combination of a very light texture and citrusy zest makes my Lemon Ice Cream a perfect complement for soft oatmeal cookies. The resulting ice cream sandwich will appeal to children and adults alike and makes a nice surprise to end a family meal. The filling can be made a day or two ahead and should be soft enough to scoop directly from the container and spread onto cookies.

Makes 8 sandwiches

16 Soft Oatmeal Cookies (page 89)
Lemon Ice Cream (page 115)

1. Make the cookies as directed. Cool completely and match up similar-size cookies to make pairs.
2. Spoon some of the ice cream onto the flat side of 1 cookie. Use an offset spatula or dull knife to spread to within ½ inch (1 cm) of the edges. Place the matching cookie on top, flat side down, and press gently until the filling spreads to the edges. Clean up the edges with the spatula if needed. Repeat with the remaining cookies.
3. Serve immediately, or put in an airtight plastic container (they can be stacked) and store in the freezer.

BANANA-SPLIT SANDWICHES

Inspired by a classic ice cream parlor favorite, these sandwiches combine the tastes of fresh banana, chocolate ice cream, marshmallows, and toasted nuts.

Makes 6 sandwiches

1 loaf or 6 mini loaves Banana Bread (page 106)
2 cups (100 g) miniature marshmallows
1¼ cups (215 g) milk chocolate chips
½ cup (120 ml) half-and-half
1 cup (240 ml) heavy or whipping cream
⅓ cup (40 g) pecans or walnuts, toasted and chopped

1. Prepare the Banana Bread as directed and allow to cool fully.
2. In a medium saucepan over low heat, combine 1½ cups (75 g) of the marshmallows, the chocolate chips, and the half-and-half. Stir until the chocolate is melted and the mixture is smooth. Remove from the heat and cool completely.
3. Whip the cream until stiff and set aside, away from the heat, until the chocolate mixture has completely cooled, then fold the whipped cream into the chocolate, along with the remaining ½ cup (25 g) of marshmallows and the nuts.
4. Cut the Banana Bread into slices a generous ½ inch (1.5 cm) thick. If you opted for the full-size loaf, cut each slice in half to form 2 rectangles. If you made mini loaves, slice each one in half horizontally.
5. Scoop the desired amount of filling onto 1 slice and use a dull knife or offset spatula to spread it across the bread. Place the matching slice on top and press gently until the filling spreads to the edges. Repeat with the remaining slices.
6. Freeze for about 1 hour, until set, then serve.

ROSE MERINGUES

While I was working in Los Angeles, a Persian colleague initiated me in the delights of rose ice cream. I've been unsuccessful in rediscovering the little specialist shop she showed me in an unfamiliar part of town and indeed haven't found any rose ice cream in London despite the many specialist shops; however, I have been delighted with the results of this recipe, which I adapted to re-create the light, fluffy texture and unique flavor that I fell in love with years ago. It's particularly heavenly when served between two Vanilla Meringues. You can find rose syrup at specialist Persian or Indian markets or sometimes in the international section of a large supermarket. If struggling, substitute 2 teaspoons rose water and increase the food coloring by a few extra drops.

Makes 8 sandwiches

16 Vanilla Meringues (page 86)
2 cups (480 ml) half-and-half
1½ cups (360 ml) heavy cream
½ cup (120 ml) milk
½ cup (100 g) granulated white sugar
4 teaspoons rose syrup
Pinch of salt
2 or 3 drops of red food coloring

1. Prepare the meringues as directed. They look especially nice with colored sprinkles scattered on top prior to baking. You can coordinate the timing so that they are drying in the oven and cooling while your rose ice cream is hardening in the freezer.
2. Ensure all the dairy ingredients are cold. In a medium or large bowl with an electric mixer, beat together all the ice cream ingredients for 1 to 2 minutes, until the sugar is dissolved. Pour into an ice cream maker and follow the manufacturer's instructions.
3. Transfer to an airtight plastic container, allowing at least ½ inch (1 cm) of empty space at the top of the container, as the mixture will expand as it freezes. Allow to freeze for at least 2 hours.
4. Match up similar-size meringues to make pairs. Scoop some rose ice cream onto the flat side of 1 meringue and spread gently to within ½ inch (1 cm) of the edge. Place the matching meringue on top, flat side down, and very gently press until the ice cream spreads to the edges. Repeat with the remaining meringues. Serve immediately.

MELON SORBET BUTTERFLIES

These melon sorbet sandwiches are just like biting into the ripe fruit itself—sweet and cold. Perfect to top off your next outdoor get-together!

Makes 6 sandwiches

Rolled Vanilla Cookie dough (page 80)
1 ripe honeydew melon, cubed
3 tablespoons fresh lemon juice (1 to 1½ lemons)
1¼ cups (250 g) superfine sugar
Pinch of black pepper

1. Prepare the cookie dough as directed, and while it is refrigerating, you can prepare the sorbet.
2. Use a food processor to blitz the melon into a puree. Add the lemon juice, sugar, and pepper and process for another 45 seconds. Transfer to an airtight plastic container and refrigerate until very cold.
3. Transfer to an ice cream maker and follow the manufacturer's instructions. Replace in the airtight plastic container and freeze for at least 2 hours before using to fill your sandwiches. The sorbet should remain easy to scoop even after freezing for longer.
4. Meanwhile, finish making and baking your cookies. Roll out the cookie dough and cut out at least 12 butterflies using a sandwich mold or shaped cookie cutter. It is wise to cut out 1 or 2 extra in case of mishaps. Bake as instructed.
5. If you are using a sandwich mold, gently stamp the pattern on half of the cookies immediately after taking them out of the oven. If not using a mold, you can create your own pattern on the wings by using the handle of a decoratively patterned spoon, the back of a miniature espresso or mustard spoon, the tines of a fork, or other kitchen implements. Take care not to press too hard.
6. Once the sorbet is sufficiently frozen, scoop the desired amount onto the flat side of 1 undecorated butterfly, distributing evenly. Use the mold or cutter placed over the cookie as a guide for adding the sorbet. If using a sandwich mold, you can use the plunger. Remove the mold and gently place a decorated cookie on top, with the decorated side facing up. Repeat with the remaining cookies.
7. Serve immediately, or quickly place in an airtight plastic container (they can be stacked) and freeze.

MARMALADE MADELEINES

These are the perfect light refreshment for informal gatherings. Their zesty flavor combines particularly well with Earl Grey tea, and the filling stays neatly where it belongs even if allowed to thaw a bit. Store-bought madeleines will work fine in a pinch, and I've found any spare Marmalade Ice Cream is right at home atop an oatmeal cookie!

Makes 16 small sandwiches (allow 2 or 3 per serving)

16 Zesty Madeleines (page 105)
Marmalade Ice Cream (page 115)

1. Make the madeleines as directed and allow to cool fully.
2. Make the ice cream as directed but don't freeze it.
3. Using a knife with a serrated blade, carefully slice each madeleine in half horizontally using a gentle sawing motion. Cover one cut side with a generous tablespoonful of the ice cream. Using an offset spatula or dull knife, spread to the edges, then place the other half on top. Repeat with the remaining madeleines.
4. Put in an airtight plastic container in a single layer and freeze for at least 1½ hours. The unfrozen ice cream mixture also keeps nicely in the fridge for a day or two (well covered) if you want to make it ahead to fill and freeze on a subsequent day.

PUMPKIN MASCARPONE SANDWICHES

The tangy taste of mascarpone ice cream makes a tasty contrast to the warm, spicy chocolate flavor and chewy texture of my Pumpkin Spice Cookies. Together they make an excellent treat for an autumn day, regardless of the weather!

Makes 6 large or 8 medium sandwiches

12 large or 16 medium Pumpkin Spice Cookies (page 95)
Mascarpone Ice Cream (page 114)

1. Make the cookies as directed and allow to cool completely.
2. Match up similar-size cookies to make pairs. Scoop some of the ice cream onto the flat side of 1 cookie. Using an offset spatula or dull knife, gently spread to within ½ inch (1 cm) of the edges. Place the matching cookie on top, flat side down, and press very gently to spread the ice cream to the edges. Repeat with the remaining cookies.
3. Serve immediately, or quickly place in an airtight plastic container in the freezer until ready to serve. If you need to stack them, place sheets of waxed paper between the layers.

KIDELICIOUS

While not every child is the same, I've found that the smaller customers at our shops tend to divide into those who like the simpler offerings, such as vanilla and chocolate, as plain as can be, and those who like the other extreme. This chapter is for the latter! So if your kids can't get enough of sweet chocolate chips, marshmallows, or candy toppings, you'll be sure to find something to elicit a "wow!" from them. And, of course, the recipes in this section will likewise delight those of us who haven't grown out of appreciating that more sometimes *is* more. When you're up for one of these recipes, you might want to keep the main dish on the lighter side to leave plenty of room for dessert!

CHOCOLATE MARSHMALLOW BROWNIES

If ever there was a recipe to please children, this is it! You can add roasted peanuts for nut lovers, including adult chocoholics. This recipe is especially quick and simple to prepare and doesn't require an ice cream maker, so it's great for when you are short on time.

Makes 4 large or 6 medium sandwiches

8 large or 12 medium Chewy Chocolate Brownies (page 82)
2 cups (100 g) miniature marshmallows
1¼ cups (215 g) milk chocolate chips
½ cup (120 ml) half-and-half
1 cup (240 ml) heavy cream
⅓ cup (40 g) roasted peanuts, chopped (optional)

1. Prepare and bake the brownie base as directed. While still warm, cut into rectangles or other desired shapes, ensuring to make pairs of the same size. Set aside to cool completely before removing from the pan.
2. In a medium saucepan over low heat, combine 1½ cups (75 g) of the marshmallows, the chocolate chips, and the half-and-half. Stir until the chocolate is melted and the mixture is smooth. Remove from the heat and cool completely.
3. Whip the cream until stiff and set aside, away from the heat, until the chocolate mixture has completely cooled, then fold the whipped cream into the chocolate mixture, along with the remaining ½ cup (25 g)of marshmallows and the peanuts.
4. Fill the brownie sandwiches, ensuring the cream mixture is applied to the flat sides that were touching the bottom of the pan. If cut into decorative shapes, use the same cutter again to guide the filling into the proper shape. Repeat with the remaining brownies.
5. Store in an airtight plastic container and freeze for at least 1 hour, until firm.

WHITE CHOCOLATE CHIP TEDDIES

These are decadent—kids and kids at heart will love 'em! The combination of choco-late chip cookie and rich vanilla ice cream makes them perfect for a birthday party or other special celebration. If you are short on time, the cookie recipe lends itself well to a wide variety of store-bought ice cream flavors, particularly vanilla or chocolate. And if you prefer a less sweet version, you can swap in semisweet chocolate chips for the white ones.

Makes 6 sandwiches

2⅔ cups (640 ml) whipping or heavy cream
½ cup (100 g) granulated white sugar
Pinch of salt
⅓ vanilla bean (optional)
1 teaspoon pure vanilla extract
White Chocolate Chip Cookie dough (page 93)

1. In a small saucepan over low heat, scald, but do not boil, ⅔ cup (160 ml) of the cream.
2. Remove from the heat and vigorously stir in the sugar and salt until dissolved. If using the vanilla bean, add it now and let soak. Allow to cool to room tempera-ture. Remove the vanilla bean, split lengthwise, scrape the seeds into the mixture, and discard the pod. Chill in the refrigerator.
3. Once cold, add the remaining 2 cups (480 ml) cream and the vanilla extract and stir. Put in an ice cream maker and follow the manufacturer's instructions. When ready, transfer to an airtight plastic container and freeze for at least 1½ hours.
4. Meanwhile, follow the directions for the cookies, spreading the batter in a 15 by 10 by 1-inch (38 by 25 by 2.5 cm) jelly-roll pan. After baking and while still quite warm, use a teddy bear–shaped cookie cutter to cut out 12 teddy shapes, cutting one right next to the other but avoiding the very edges of the pan, which tend to be crunchier. Let cool until slightly warm, then carefully remove to a rack and let cool completely.
5. When completely cool, replace the cutter over 1 cookie, flat side up. Cover with some of the ice cream, using an offset spatula to ensure it spreads across the entire shape. Remove the cutter and cover the ice cream with a second cookie, flat side down. Press very gently just until it adheres. Repeat with the remaining cookies.
6. Serve immediately, or freeze in airtight plastic containers. If you must stack the sandwiches, use waxed paper between the layers.

S'MORE SANDWICHES

I first discovered s'mores as a child while staying at a friend's family cabin in a redwood forest in California. They're a delicious treat, traditionally made over a campfire, and part of the fun is in taking your time to roast the marshmallow evenly. Although this recipe has all your favorite ingredients for the real thing, you won't need a campfire to enjoy these! If you can't find mini marshmallows, regular-size ones can be cut into quarters so that the assembled sandwiches are still thin enough to eat comfortably.

Makes 6 sandwiches

Chewy Chocolate Brownie dough (page 82)
7 or 8 or graham cracker halves
Chocolate Ice Cream (page 112), or 1 pint (480 ml) premium store-bought
¾ cup (40 g) mini marshmallows

1. Preheat the oven to 350°F (180°C). Spread the brownie dough in the pan as directed.
2. Before popping the pan into the oven, break up the graham crackers into 8 to 10 pieces each and divide them evenly over the batter. Gently push into the batter slightly so that they will remain attached once the batter is baked. Bake as directed.
3. While still warm from the oven, cut the brownies into 12 uniform rectangles. Let cool for at least 10 minutes before removing from the pan.
4. Allow the ice cream to soften slightly, then spoon one-sixth of it onto the under-side of 1 brownie. Using an offset spatula or dull knife, spread it evenly to within about ¼ inch (5 mm) of the edges. Place 10 to 12 mini marshmallows on top. Add the second brownie, bottom side down, and press gently until the ice cream spreads to the edges. Repeat with the remaining brownies.
5. Serve immediately, or freeze in an airtight plastic container. If you need to stack the sandwiches, place sheets of waxed paper between the layers.

PEANUT BUTTER BITES

For a classic American combination of flavors, nothing beats peanut butter and chocolate. These are especially decadent due to the chocolate chips in the cookies themselves, so I recommend they be made small.

Makes 6 bite-size sandwiches

Tin Roof Cookie dough (page 101)
Butter, for greasing
Flour, for flattening
Chocolate Ice Cream (page 112), or 1 pint (480 ml) premium store-bought
½ cup (75 g) chocolate sprinkles

1. Prepare the cookie dough as directed. Grease a cookie sheet. Drop small, even amounts (about 1 level tablespoonful) approximately 3 inches (7.5 cm) apart on the greased cookie sheet. Use the flat bottom of a glass (dipped each time in flour) to flatten to about ½ inch (1 cm) high.
2. Bake as directed for 7 to 8 minutes, just until the cookies are starting to turn golden on the edges. Cool completely on a wire rack.
3. If using my ice cream recipe, make it as directed but do not freeze it. Pair up similar-size cookies, spread the desired amount of ice cream on the flat side of 1 cookie (the side that was touching the cookie sheet), and gently place the second cookie on top, flat side down. Press until the filling spreads to the edges.
4. Spread the sprinkles on a plate with edges. Gently roll the sides of the sandwich in the sprinkles so that they stick to the filling. Repeat with the remaining cookies.
5. If using store-bought ice cream, the sandwiches may be served immediately. If using homemade, freeze for at least 1½ hours before serving. To store, place in an airtight plastic container. The sandwiches may be stacked, but the sides must not touch.

CHOCOLATE CANDY CRUSH

You may find that only the young will have the appetite to finish off this indulgent combination of cookie, ice cream, and chocolate candy bar . . . or you may be surprised! Either way, with the rich combination, I recommend making the cookies on the smaller side. Note that the chocolate will adhere much better if it is finely chopped and the ice cream is neither too soft nor rock hard.

Makes 6 sandwiches

12 Soft Oatmeal Cookies (page 89)
3 regular-size chocolate candy bars, such as Snickers, Mars, or Heath, finely chopped
    or crushed
Vanilla Ice Cream (page 112), or 1 pint (480 ml) premium store-bought

1. Make the cookies as directed. Once they are fully cooled, pair up similar-size cookies. Put the candy bars on a rimmed plate or shallow bowl.
2. Spread a ¾-inch (2 cm) layer of firm ice cream onto the flat side of 1 cookie. Using an offset spatula, pat the ice cream down evenly until it nearly spreads to the edges. Place a second cookie, flat side down, on top and press down gently until the ice cream starts to extend beyond the rim.
3. Quickly roll the edges of the sandwich in the candy pieces until they are covered. While filling and rolling the remaining sandwiches, store those already made in the freezer, as they will melt more quickly with the chocolate coating.
4. Serve immediately, or keep in an airtight plastic container in the freezer until ready to enjoy. If you need to stack them, place sheets of waxed paper between the layers. If frozen, allow to sit for 3 minutes before serving.

MARMALADE BEAR SANDWICHES

Inspired by Paddington, the iconic bear from the children's tales who sure likes his marmalade sandwiches, you'll love these bear-shaped chocolate brownie sandwiches with marmalade ice cream filling! Kids tend to like them better if you call it orange ice cream, as some of them have a prejudice against marmalade due to its texture.

Makes 6 sandwiches

Chewy Chocolate Brownie dough (page 82)
Marmalade Ice Cream (page 115)

1. Prepare the brownie base as directed. While still warm, cut into shapes using a teddy bear–shaped cookie cutter. Set aside to cool completely.
2. Make the ice cream as directed, but do not freeze.
3. Scoop the desired amount of ice cream onto the underside of 1 brownie. With an offset spatula, gently spread the ice cream evenly outward toward the edges. (Use your clean cookie cutter over the brownie as a guide.) Wipe the back of the spatula before evening out the "walls" of the ice cream. Gently place another brownie, bottom side down, on top. Repeat with the remaining brownies.
4. Store in an airtight plastic container, being careful that the sides don't touch, and freeze for at least 1 hour, until firm. If you need to stack the sandwiches, place sheets of waxed paper between the layers.

FESTIVE

In this section, you will find ideas to make special occasions stand out with themed ice cream sandwiches. Try Mint Chip Valentines (page 62) for your loved ones in February or, for something unique at Halloween, take a crack at Graveyard Coffins (page 77). Complete with gummy worms spilling out the sides, they'll be sure to please even teens too cool to dress up.

What better way to celebrate than with Chocolate Chip Stars (page 72)? And Christmas provides several opportunities for festive sandwiches: Flocked Trees (page 68), sandwiches decorated to look like drums (page 64), or the sophisticated Fruitcake Delights (page 74) will please your December guests.

MINT CHIP VALENTINES

What better way to show your love on Valentine's Day or any other time of year? Refreshing mint ice cream paired with a chewy brownie base makes a winning combination. Store-bought mint–chocolate chip ice cream works well, but if you can't find it or prefer your own homemade ice cream, you can swirl a couple of spoonfuls of crème de menthe liqueur and ⅓ cup (30 g) of chocolate flakes into vanilla ice cream.

Makes 4 large or 6 medium sandwiches

Chewy Chocolate Brownie dough (page 82)
1 pint (480 ml) store-bought mint–chocolate chip ice cream
4 ounces (115 g) semisweet chocolate
¼ cup (60 ml) mini chocolate chips, flakes, or chocolate sprinkles, to decorate (optional)

1. Make the brownie base as directed. As soon as you take the pan out of the oven, use a heart-shaped cookie cutter to cut shapes, but do not remove from the pan. Use all of the available surface, taking care not to overlap.
2. Once you've finished cutting, set the pan on a rack to cool. Take the ice cream out of the freezer to soften. Set a timer for 10 minutes to check its progress.
3. Make the topping by melting the semisweet chocolate in a small heatproof bowl in the microwave on 80 percent power for 45 seconds, then stirring well. Repeat for further periods of 20 seconds at a time until fully melted, stirring after each interval. Alternatively, put the heatproof bowl over a pan of hot (not boiling) water and stir until completely melted. Set aside to cool while you assemble the hearts.
4. Once the brownie shapes are cool, use a flat spatula to lift them carefully onto your work surface. Scoop the desired amount of ice cream onto the underside of 1 brownie. With an offset spatula, gently spread the ice cream evenly outward toward the edges. (Use your clean cookie cutter over the brownie as a guide.) Wipe the back of the spatula before evening out the "walls" of the ice cream. Gently place another brownie heart, bottom side down, on top.
5. Working quickly, dip half the assembled sandwich (bow to tip) into the melted chocolate. Avoid letting it sit too long or the ice cream will melt. If a thicker coat is desired, let the first coat harden before you redip. Before the chocolate dip hardens, sprinkle on the mini chips. While filling and dipping the remaining sandwiches, store those already made in the freezer, as they will melt more quickly with the chocolate coating.
6. Place the sandwiches, without stacking, in an airtight plastic container and freeze for at least 20 minutes, until firm, before serving.

MERRY DRUMS

When you've got guests during the Christmas season, these sandwiches will help to set the scene and make for a festive occasion. You can substitute your favorite ice cream to fill them. Because of the sweetness of the icing, you may find that a more tangy flavor, such as mascarpone, lemon, or orange, provides the best balance. If you don't have a circular cookie cutter, use the rim of a glass as a guide, cutting around it with the tip of a dull knife.

Makes 6 sandwiches

Rolled Vanilla Cookie dough (page 80; there will be some left over)
Butter, for greasing
Flour, for rolling
Mascarpone Ice Cream (page 114), or 1 pint (480 ml) flavor of your choice
¼ cup (30 g) confectioners' sugar, for rolling
1 pound (450 g) fondant

For the drum decorations
1 to 2 fruit-flavored rolls, such as Betty Crocker Fruit Roll-Ups, red or green
12 pretzel sticks
12 small gumdrops

1. Make the cookie dough as directed and divide in half. Flatten each half into a disk. Wrap in plastic wrap and chill for at least 30 minutes.
2. Preheat the oven to 350°F (180°C). Grease a cookie sheet. With a rolling pin, roll out 1 disk of chilled dough at a time on a floured surface into a round about ¼ inch (5 mm) thick.
3. Using a round cookie cutter, cut out an even number of cookies 2½ to 3 inches in diameter. Repeat with the remaining dough, rerolling scraps as needed. You will need 12 rounds in all for the sandwiches. You can use any extra dough to make extra cookies or freeze it for another time.
4. Space the cookies at least ½ inch (1 cm) apart on the cookie sheet and bake for 6 to 9 minutes, until the edges are just starting to brown. Cool completely on a wire rack.

5. Allow the ice cream to soften while preparing the icing. On a surface sprinkled with confectioners' sugar, roll out about half of the fondant until about ¼ inch (5 mm) thick. Cut out strips of fondant using a straight edge to ensure an even width. The width should match the thickness of your finished ice cream sandwiches; this will depend on the desired thickness of the ice cream layer, but should be about 1¼ inches (3 cm).

6. Use the same cutter or guide that you used for the cookies to cut 12 circles in the remaining fondant. Set aside.

7. Apply a layer of softened ice cream about ¾ inch (2 cm) thick to the flat side of 1 cookie. Smooth the edges with an offset spatula or dull knife and add a second cookie, flat side down.

8. Quickly apply fondant circles to the top and bottom of the ice cream sandwich, moistening them slightly with water if needed to help them adhere, then apply a long strip around the edges to join them. (You can do this by rolling the sandwich along the strip and cutting off any extra to use for the next sandwich.)

9. As the sandwiches are made, put them, without stacking and with their sides not touching, in an airtight plastic container and place in the freezer if not eating right away.

For the drum decorations

1. Unroll the fruit roll and cut strips 1¾ to 2 inches (4.5 to 5 cm) long. Lightly moisten one side of each strip with water and apply in a zigzag fashion around the sides of the drums.

2. Insert each pretzel stick into the (flat) bottom of a gumdrop to form drumsticks. Just before serving, lay 2 drumsticks, crossing them, on top of each sandwich (the pretzel drumsticks should not be frozen).

FLOCKED TREES

These make an inventive alternative to Christmas cookies for when guests come 'round. And if you have children, they'll be more than happy to pitch in with the decoration of the cookies, especially if they're allowed to sample! As the icing needs time to dry, you are best off making and decorating the cookies a day ahead. You can follow the instructions as below or use a Christmas-tree cookie cutter if available.

Makes 6 sandwiches

Rolled Vanilla Cookie dough (page 80)
Butter, for greasing
Flour, for rolling
¾ cup (90 g) confectioners' sugar
Few drops of pure almond extract
Few drops of green food coloring
Colored sprinkles, colored sugar, or other edible decorations
1 pint (480 ml) ice cream, flavor of your choice

1. Make the cookie dough as directed and divide in half. Flatten each half into a disk. Wrap in plastic wrap and chill for at least 30 minutes.
2. Preheat the oven to 350°F (180°C). Grease 2 cookie sheets. With a rolling pin, roll out 1 disk of chilled dough at a time on a floured surface into a round about ¼ inch (5 mm) thick.
3. Use a Christmas-tree cutter measuring 4 to 5 inches (10 to 13 cm) tall. Or, if you don't have one, cut out a perfect circle about 8 inches (20 cm) in diameter with the tip of a dull knife. You can use the rim of a mixing bowl as a guide. Remove the bowl and cut all the way across the diameter of the circle, through the center. Make two more cuts like this, equally spaced, so that you have six equally sized triangles (with rounded bottom edges).
4. Repeat with the remaining dough, then space the shapes at least ½ inch (1 cm) apart on the cookie sheets and bake for about 8 minutes, until the edges are just starting to brown. Remove from the sheets and cool.
5. Prepare the icing by mixing the confectioners' sugar with the almond extract and green coloring, then stir in water a few drops at a time until you have a consistency that is thick but still workable.

6. Either drizzle or pipe the icing onto the top side of half the triangles in a zigzag pattern, starting at the tree top. Immediately sprinkle with your chosen decoration (it will only stick to the icing within a minute of applying it to the cookie). If you sprinkle either over a bowl or on parchment paper, you can capture the fallen sprinkles and reuse them on another cookie.

7. Allow the icing to dry for at least 1 hour before assembling the ice cream sandwiches, although overnight is better.

8. Allow the ice cream to soften, then apply a layer about ¾ inch (2 cm) thick to the bottom of a non-iced cookie. Smooth the edges with an offset spatula or dull knife and carefully (holding its edges) add an iced and decorated cookie, with the undecorated side facing down. Repeat with the remaining cookies.

9. Serve immediately, or freeze, without stacking and with their sides not touching, in airtight plastic containers.

CHOCOLATE CHIP STARS

When it's time for celebration, serve up quintessential chocolate-chip ice cream sandwiches cut into star shapes. For more spark, you can add colored sprinkles to the edges. If you don't have mini chips on hand, simply chop regular-size chips, but be sure to measure by volume after chopping. These can also be made with an ice cream sandwich mold instead of a cookie cutter.

Makes 6 sandwiches

2⅔ cups (640 ml) whipping or heavy cream
½ cup (100 g) granulated white sugar
Pinch of salt
⅓ vanilla bean (optional)
1 teaspoon pure vanilla extract
½ cup (85 g) mini chocolate chips
12 All-American Chocolate Chip Cookies (page 88)
Colored sprinkles, for decorating (optional)

1. In a small saucepan over low heat, scald, but do not boil, ⅔ cup (160 ml) of the cream. Remove from the heat and vigorously stir in the sugar and salt until dissolved. If using the vanilla bean, add it now and let soak. Allow the mixture to come to room temperature. Remove the vanilla bean, split lengthwise, scrape the seeds into the mixture, and discard the pod. Chill in the refrigerator.

2. Once cold, add the remaining 2 cups (480 ml) of cream and the vanilla extract and stir. Put in an ice cream maker and follow the manufacturer's instructions. When nearly ready except for the final few rotations, drop in the mini chocolate chips. Once ready, transfer to an airtight plastic container and freeze for at least 1½ hours.

3. Meanwhile, make the cookies as directed. After baking and while still quite warm, use a star-shaped cookie cutter to cut out an even number of star shapes, fitting one right next to the other but avoiding the very edges of the pan, which tend to be crunchier. After cutting all of them, let them cool until slightly warm, then cool on a rack.

4. Turn 1 cookie flat side up and replace the cutter over it. Cover with ice cream, using a small offset spatula to ensure it spreads across the entire shape. Remove the cutter and cover the ice cream with a second cookie, flat side down. Press very gently just until it adheres. Repeat with the rest of the cookies.

5. Shake sprinkles onto the edges and serve immediately, or freeze in airtight plastic containers. If you must stack, use waxed paper between the layers.

FRUITCAKE DELIGHTS

Christmas fruitcake has been enjoyed by generations during the festive season. The cookies used here, packed with toasted hazelnuts, pecans, and walnuts as well as candied fruits, incorporate the best bits but leave aside the less universally popular ingredients like rum and golden raisins. Filled with Marmalade Ice Cream, these bite-size gems (pictured on page 103) make a festive treat that's easy to enjoy even while mingling at a gathering.

Makes 24 mini sandwiches

48 Fruitcake Cookies (page 102)
Marmalade Ice Cream (page 115)

1. Make the cookies as directed. Once completely cool, remove and discard the paper liner from each cookie.
2. Make the ice cream as directed but do not freeze it.
3. Place a small dollop of filling on the flat side of a cookie and gently place a second cookie on top, flat side down. Repeat with the remaining cookies.
4. Store—without stacking—in an airtight plastic container and freeze for at least 1½ hours before serving.

CELEBRATION CAKE SANDWICHES

What could be better for a birthday or other special celebration than ice cream, cake and buttercream all rolled into one? You can substitute six slices of Banana Bread (page 106) or even your favorite loaf cake for a children's party treat.

Makes 6 sandwiches

6 slices Mocha Loaf (page 108)
4 tablespoons (60 g) butter, at room temperature
2 to 2¼ cups (230 to 260 g) confectioners' sugar
2 tablespoons milk, at room temperature
½ teaspoon pure vanilla extract
Few drops of food coloring (optional)
1 pint (480 ml) ice cream, flavor of your choice
2 tablespoons colored or chocolate sprinkles, for decorating (optional)

1. Make the Mocha Loaf as directed and allow to cool fully before slicing.
2. Meanwhile, prepare the buttercream. In a small bowl, use an electric mixer to beat the butter with the confectioners' sugar at low speed until incorporated. Scrape down the sides of the bowl, add the milk and vanilla extract, and beat at medium–high speed until light and fluffy. Set aside.
3. If you wish the tops of the sandwiches to be decorated, set aside a portion of buttercream and add a few drops of your desired food coloring, mixing with a fork to incorporate. Load the colored icing into a pastry bag with an icing nozzle if you wish to pipe a design or message.
4. Allow the ice cream to soften at room temperature. With an offset spatula, apply a thin layer of buttercream to one side of each slice of the Mocha Loaf, then cut each slice in half crosswise. Apply a generous layer of ice cream on top of the buttercream on a half slice. Place the matching half, buttercream side down, on top of the ice cream. If desired, spread the colored buttercream on top or pipe a message or pattern. (The sandwiches will be easier to eat if you keep the icing on top just in the center.) Add sprinkles if desired; they will help prevent the icing from smearing or running. Repeat with the remaining slices.
5. Serve immediately, or quickly place in an airtight plastic container, without stacking, and freeze.

GRAVEYARD COFFINS

Sure to delight children and adults at your next Halloween party, these scary coffins are easier to make than you might think! You can make your own writing icing by combining ¼ cup (30 g) of confectioners' sugar with a few drops of water and stirring until very smooth. Use to fill a bag with a writing nozzle, or in a pinch, use a strong resealable, plastic bag with a very small hole snipped off one corner.

Makes 5 sandwiches

10 Chewy Chocolate Brownies (page 82)
Chocolate Ice Cream (page 112), or 1 pint (480 ml) premium store-bought, softened
20 gummy worms or gummy body parts
1 tube white writing icing

1. Bake the brownie base as directed. While still warm from the oven, cut into 10 uniform rectangles. Avoid using the very edges that are touching the sides of the pan, which tend to be crunchier.
2. Match up rectangles, placing them bottom side to bottom side. Cut off the corners, following the basic shape shown in the photo opposite.
3. Spread the desired amount of softened ice cream onto the bottom of 1 coffin brownie. Smooth the edges with an offset spatula or a dull knife. Place 4 gummy sweets across the ice cream so that they are sticking out over the edge of the coffin.
4. Smooth a very thin layer of ice cream on the bottom side of the matching coffin brownie and quickly put it over the ice cream and the gummy sweets. Repeat with the remaining brownies.
5. Quickly place the sandwiches in an airtight plastic container—without stacking—and freeze until ready to serve. Just before serving, use the writing icing to pipe your desired "epitaph" onto each coffin, such as R.I.P. or "Here lies" and your guest's name!

THE COOKIE RECIPES

Here are cookie ideas to complement almost any season or occasion. Why not try a light and crunchy Vanilla Meringue (page 86) or a moist and tender Grated Apple Cookie (page 91)? Both of these combine well with creamy or fruity fillings. And for coconut lovers, nothing beats a chunky Coconut Macaroon (page 96), which, paired with a chocolate ice cream, will satiate the most ardent craving.

This section also presents a few alternatives to conventional cookies: trendy madeleines, much-loved Banana Bread (page 106), and a sophisticated Mocha Loaf (page 108). Although these alternatives can be frozen, you may find it best to make, slice, and fill them right before serving,

Whichever your predilection, you will find something here to go perfectly with your favorite ice cream or sorbet.

ROLLED VANILLA COOKIES

Makes 16 to 24 cookies

1 cup (225 g) butter, at room temperature
½ cup (110 g) firmly packed light brown sugar
½ cup (100 g) granulated white sugar
1 extra-large egg
1½ teaspoons pure vanilla extract
5½ teaspoons milk
2½ cups (350 g) all-purpose flour, plus extra for rolling
1 teaspoon baking powder
Colored sugar or sprinkles, for decorating (optional)

> **NOTE:** If you wish to substitute pure almond extract for vanilla, decrease to 1 teaspoon and increase the milk to 2 tablespoons.

1. In a large bowl, use an electric mixer with the beaters or paddle to cream the butter. Add both types of sugar and the egg and mix until creamy.
2. Beat in the vanilla extract and milk and continue beating until well mixed. Add the flour and baking powder and beat on low speed until well incorporated.
3. Divide the dough in half; flatten each half to about ½ inch (1 cm) thick. Cover in plastic wrap and refrigerate until firm (about 2 hours).
4. Preheat the oven to 400°F (200°C). Lightly grease 2 cookie sheets. One disk at a time, roll out the dough on a lightly floured surface until ½ inch (1 cm) thick. Cut with the desired shape of cutter. Wiggle the cutter slightly to ensure a clean outline. Place the cookies 1 inch (2.5 cm) apart on the cookie sheets. At this stage, colored sugar or sprinkles may be added to the unbaked cookies; press it on lightly.
5. Bake for 6 to 9 minutes, until the edges are just lightly browned. Immediately remove from the cookie sheet to a cooling rack and allow to cool completely before filling or storing in an airtight container.

CHEWY CHOCOLATE BROWNIES

Makes 8 to 12 brownies

½ cup (115 g) butter or margarine, plus extra for greasing
2 ounces (60 g) unsweetened baking chocolate, 90 percent cacao (see tip)
1 cup (200 g) granulated white sugar
2 extra-large eggs
1½ teaspoons pure vanilla extract
½ cup (70 g) all-purpose flour
Pinch of salt

1. Preheat the oven to 350°F (180°C). Lightly grease a 15 by 10 by 1-inch (38 by 25 by 2.5 cm) jelly-roll pan.
2. Put the butter and chocolate in a heatproof bowl. Microwave on 70 percent power for 1 minute. Stir together and repeat until completely melted. Alternatively, you can melt the two ingredients in a heatproof bowl set over a pan of simmering water (not boiling), stirring until melted.
3. Add the sugar to the chocolate mixture and stir. Allow to cool slightly, then add the eggs and vanilla, stirring with a fork until completely incorporated. Add the flour and salt and stir until just incorporated.
4. Spread the batter evenly across the greased pan, using an offset spatula or the back of a spoon to ensure it is evenly distributed. Any other ingredients that are to be baked in the batter (for example, the graham crackers in the s'mores on page 53) should be added now.
5. Bake for 10 to 12 minutes. The center should be firm but still slightly moist and the edges *may* start to pull away from the sides of the pan. Do not overcook. Remove from the oven and cut with a knife or use shaped cutters immediately, while still hot. Allow to cool before filling or storing in an airtight container.

TIP: Using chocolate with 90 percent cacao makes these brownies really dark and chocolaty. If you can't find it and your chocolate has a lower percentage, add 2 tablespoons cocoa powder in place of the chocolate and reduce the sugar by 2 tablespoons.

BUTTERSCOTCH BROWNIES

Makes 8 to 12 brownies

4 tablespoons (60 g) butter, plus extra for greasing
1 cup (220 g) firmly packed light brown sugar
1 extra-large egg
1½ teaspoons pure vanilla extract
¾ cup (110 g) all-purpose flour
¾ teaspoon baking powder
¼ teaspoon baking soda
¼ teaspoon salt
¾ cup (150 g) finely chopped dates (12 to 14 dates), sprinkled with 1 tablespoon flour
    to prevent sticking (see tip)

1. Preheat the oven to 350°F (180°C). Grease a 9-inch (23 cm) square baking pan.
2. In a small heatproof bowl, melt the butter in the microwave, using 80 percent power for 20 to 30 seconds. Alternatively, put the heatproof bowl over a pan of hot (not boiling) water and stir until completely melted. Stir in the brown sugar until dissolved. Allow to cool slightly, then beat in the egg and vanilla extract with a hand whisk until well incorporated.
3. In a separate bowl, whisk together the flour, baking powder, baking soda, and salt. Gradually stir into the sugar mixture, then stir in the dates. Spread into the greased pan, using an offset spatula or the back of a spoon to ensure it is evenly distributed.
4. Bake for 18 to 20 minutes, until a toothpick inserted into the center comes out clean. Cut into your desired shapes while still warm. Allow to cool before filling or storing in an airtight container.

TIP: If your dates are not very moist, cut into bits and put into a small pan along with 2 tablespoons water. Cook over low heat, stirring constantly, until they form a soft paste. Cool before adding to the mixture as directed and omit the 1 tablespoon flour.

SNICKERDOODLE COOKIES

Makes 12 cookies

Dough
1½ cups (210 g) all-purpose flour
1 teaspoon baking powder
¼ teaspoon salt
½ cup (115 g) butter, at room temperature
½ cup (100 g) granulated white sugar
¼ cup (55 g) firmly packed light brown sugar
1 extra-large egg
¾ teaspoon pure vanilla extract

Coating
⅓ cup (65 g) granulated white sugar
2 teaspoons ground cinnamon

Flour or confectioners' sugar, if needed

1. To make the dough, in a large bowl whisk together the flour, baking powder, and salt. Using an electric mixer with the beaters or paddle, in a separate bowl beat together the butter and sugars until smooth (about 3 minutes). Stop the mixer and scrape down the sides of the bowl once or twice as necessary.

2. Add the egg, beating well, then beat in the vanilla extract. Add the flour mixture in two batches, beating until smooth. Cover and refrigerate until firm enough to roll into balls (45 to 60 minutes).

3. Preheat the oven to 400°F (200°C). Place a rack in the center of the oven and line 2 cookie sheets with parchment paper. For the coating, mix together the sugar and cinnamon in a small bowl.

4. Shape the dough into 1¼-inch (3 cm) balls, then roll the balls in the coating mixture one at a time and place on the prepared sheets about 3 inches (7.5 cm) apart. Using the bottom of a glass, gently flatten each cookie evenly to about ½ inch (1 cm) thick. If the cookies begin to stick to the glass, lightly coat the glass in flour or confectioners' sugar.

5. Bake the cookies for 8 to 10 minutes, until the edges are light golden brown. Remove from the oven, wait for 1 minute, and, using a spatula, place on a wire rack to cool. These cookies can be stored in an airtight container at room temperature for about 1 week.

VANILLA MERINGUES

Makes 16 meringues

3 extra-large egg whites
Pinch of salt
¼ teaspoon cream of tartar
1 cup (200 g) granulated white sugar
½ teaspoon distilled white vinegar or fresh lemon juice
1½ teaspoons pure vanilla extract
Assorted colored sprinkles, for decorating (optional)

For chocolate meringues (optional)
1 tablespoon cocoa powder
½ cup (85 g) chocolate chips, ideally semisweet

1. Using an electric mixer with the whisk attachment, beat the egg whites and salt in a large bowl until frothy. Add the cream of tartar and continue beating as you lightly sprinkle the sugar over the egg whites until it is completely added. Add the vinegar, vanilla extract, and, if making chocolate meringues, the cocoa powder. Beat until stiff peaks form and the mixture is glossy.
2. Line 2 cookie sheets with parchment paper and preheat the oven to 200 to 210°F (95 to 100°C).
3. Fit a pastry bag with a large-mouthed nozzle in your desired shape (a smooth, round nozzle works well). If you don't have a pastry bag and icing nozzle, you can use a large resealable plastic bag and snip a small hole (about ½ inch / 1 cm) across one bottom corner.
4. Pipe meringues onto the lined cookie sheets in spirals, starting in the center and working outward until each one is about 3 inches in diameter, using all the meringue mixture. Be sure to allow a bit of space between the meringues, as they expand slightly in the oven. Apply sprinkle decorations or, if making chocolate meringues, the chocolate chips, pressing the chips gently to ensure they adhere.
5. Bake for 2 to 2½ hours. After this time, do not remove from the oven, but turn the oven off, leaving the door closed and the meringues inside until completely cooled. You can leave them in the oven overnight if you wish. Use as required or store the meringues in an airtight container.

ALL-AMERICAN CHOCOLATE CHIP COOKIES

Makes 8 to 12 cookies

1 cup (225 g) butter, at room temperature, plus extra for greasing

1 cup (220 g) firmly packed light brown sugar

½ cup (100 g) granulated white sugar

2 extra-large eggs

1½ teaspoons pure vanilla extract

2¼ cups (315 g) all-purpose flour

1 teaspoon salt

1 teaspoon baking soda

2 cups (340 g) semisweet chocolate chips

1. Preheat the oven to 350°F (180°C). Lightly grease a 15 by 10 by 1-inch (38 by 25 by 2.5 cm) jelly-roll pan.

2. In a bowl, use an electric mixer with the beaters or paddle to cream the butter. Add both sugars and mix until light and fluffy. Beat in the eggs and vanilla extract. Sift in the flour, salt, and baking soda and stir to incorporate.

3. Stir in the chocolate chips, then spread the batter evenly across the greased pan, using an offset spatula or the back of a spoon to ensure it is evenly distributed.

4. Bake for 12 to 15 minutes. The edges should look golden and the center should appear firm. Do not overcook. Remove from the oven and, while still warm, immediately use shaped cutters to cut through the cookie dough. Jiggle the cutter slightly to achieve a clean line. Remove the cutouts when cooled. Use as required or store in an airtight container.

SOFT OATMEAL COOKIES

Makes 16 cookies

½ cup (115 g) butter, at room temperature
¾ cup (165 g) firmly packed light brown sugar
¼ cup (50 g) granulated white sugar
1 extra-large egg
1 teaspoon pure vanilla extract
1 tablespoon milk
1 cup (140 g) all-purpose flour
½ teaspoon baking powder
½ teaspoon baking soda
½ teaspoon salt
1 cup (75 g) old-fashioned rolled oats
1 teaspoon ground cinnamon
½ teaspoon ground nutmeg, allspice, or pumpkin pie spice (optional)
½ cup raisins, nuts, chocolate chips, dried coconut, or a combination (optional)

1. Preheat the oven to 350°F (180°C).
2. In a large bowl, use an electric mixer with the beaters or paddle to cream the butter. Add both sugars and mix until creamy. Beat in the egg, vanilla extract, and milk and continue beating until well mixed.
3. Add the flour, baking powder, baking soda, and salt. Beat on low speed until well incorporated.
4. Add the oats, cinnamon, and any desired spices and/or other optional ingredients and mix on low speed just until incorporated.
5. Using a small ice cream scoop if possible (or measuring out 2 tablespoons per cookie), drop heaps of the mixture 1½ inches (4 cm) apart onto ungreased cookie sheets. Aim to use the same amount for each cookie so that they will match up in pairs.
6. Bake for 9 to 11 minutes, until the edges are just lightly browned. Immediately remove from the cookie sheet to a cooling rack and allow to cool completely before filling or storing in an airtight container.

GRATED APPLE COOKIES

Makes 12 large cookies

4 tablespoons (60 g) butter, at room temperature, plus extra for greasing
⅔ cup (150 g) firmly packed light brown sugar
1 extra-large egg
1 teaspoon pure vanilla extract
1 cup (140 g) all-purpose flour
½ teaspoon baking powder
¼ teaspoon baking soda
¼ teaspoon salt
¾ teaspoon ground cinnamon
¼ teaspoon ground nutmeg
2 tablespoons apple juice
Scant ½ cup (50 g) walnuts, lightly toasted and chopped
½ cup (60 g) raisins (optional)
½ cup (95 g) grated tart apple, such as Granny Smith (about 1 apple)

1. Preheat the oven to 400°F (200°C). Grease a couple of cookie sheets.
2. In a large bowl, use an electric mixer with the beaters or paddle to cream the butter and sugar together until well combined. Beat in the egg and vanilla extract until well mixed.
3. In a separate bowl, whisk together the flour, baking powder, baking soda, salt, cinnamon, and nutmeg. Add to the creamed mixture in three batches, alternating with additions of the apple juice. Stir in the walnuts, raisins, and apple. Drop by teaspoons onto the greased cookie sheets, leaving 1½ to 2 inches (4 to 5 cm) between the cookies.
4. Bake for 9 to 11 minutes, until golden brown. Immediately remove from the cookie sheet to a cooling rack and allow to cool completely before filling or storing in an airtight container.

SOFT GINGER COOKIES

Makes 16 cookies

6 tablespoons (90 g) butter, at room temperature
1 cup (200 g) granulated white sugar
1 extra-large egg
¼ cup (60 ml) light molasses
2 cups (280 g) all-purpose flour
2 teaspoons baking soda
½ teaspoon salt
1½ teaspoons ground ginger
1¼ teaspoons ground cinnamon

1. In a large bowl, use an electric mixer with the beaters or paddle to cream the butter and ⅔ cup (135 g) of the sugar until well combined. Beat in the egg and molasses until well combined.
2. In a separate bowl, stir together the flour, baking soda, salt, ginger, and cinnamon. Add the flour mixture to the butter mixture and beat until combined. Refrigerate the dough for 2 hours.
3. Preheat the oven to 350°F (180°C). Roll the dough into balls about 1½ inches (4 cm) in diameter. Put the remaining ⅓ cup (65 g) of sugar in a shallow bowl. Roll the balls in the sugar and arrange about 2 inches (5 cm) apart on ungreased cookie sheets. Use the bottom of a glass to flatten each cookie to about 3¼ inches (8 cm) in diameter. If the cookies begin to stick to the glass, lightly coat the glass in flour or confectioners' sugar.
4. Bake for 7 to 8 minutes, until the cookies are puffed and the tops are cracked. Remove immediately to a cooling rack, allowing space between the cookies; they will flatten as they cool. Once cool, use as required or store in an airtight container.

WHITE CHOCOLATE CHIP COOKIES

Makes 8 to 12 cookies

¾ cup (180 g) butter, at room temperature, plus extra for greasing

1 cup (220 g) firmly packed light brown sugar

½ cup (100 g) granulated white sugar

2 extra-large eggs

1 teaspoon pure vanilla extract

2¼ cups (350 g) all-purpose flour

1 teaspoon salt

1 teaspoon baking soda

2 cups (340 g) white chocolate chips

1. Preheat the oven to 350°F (180°C).
2. In a medium bowl, use an electric mixer with the beaters or paddle to cream the butter. Add both sugars and mix until light and fluffy. Beat in the eggs and vanilla extract. Sift in the flour, salt, and baking soda and mix to incorporate. Stir in the chocolate chips.
3. If you want to make cutout shapes, lightly grease a 15 by 10 by 1-inch (38 by 25 by 2.5 cm) jelly-roll pan. Spread the dough evenly across the pan with an offset spatula. Bake for 10 to 12 minutes, until the center is cooked and the edges are only lightly browned. Remove from the oven and, while still hot, cut into shapes with your desired cutter.
4. For round cookies, lightly grease a cookie sheet. Drop even amounts of the dough (about 2 tablespoons) from a small ice cream scoop, spacing them at least 1½ inches (4 cm) apart. Bake for 8 to 10 minutes, until the center is cooked and the edges are only lightly browned. Be careful not to overcook. Allow to cool completely before filling or storing in an airtight container.

PUMPKIN SPICE COOKIES

Makes 12 to 16 cookies

½ cup (40 g) old-fashioned rolled oats
1 cup (140 g) all-purpose flour
½ teaspoon baking soda
¼ teaspoon salt
1 teaspoon ground cinnamon
¼ teaspoon ground nutmeg
½ cup (115 g) butter, at room temperature, plus extra for greasing
½ cup (110 g) firmly packed light brown sugar
6 tablespoons (75 g) granulated white sugar
1 extra-large egg, lightly beaten
½ teaspoon pure vanilla extract
½ cup (120 g) canned pumpkin puree
½ cup (85 g) semisweet chocolate chips

> **NOTE:** Canned pumpkin puree is concentrated; if substituting homemade pumpkin puree, ensure you have drained off as much moisture as possible by sieving and packing down.

1. Preheat the oven to 350°F (180°C). Grease a couple of cookie sheets.
2. In a bowl, combine the oats, flour, baking soda, salt, cinnamon, and nutmeg. In another large bowl, use an electric mixer to cream the butter, then gradually add both sugars. Beat until light and fluffy; this takes 2 to 3 minutes. Add the egg and vanilla extract and incorporate well.
3. Add the dry ingredients in three batches alternately with the pumpkin puree in two batches, beginning and ending with the dry ingredients and mixing well after each addition. Stir in the chocolate chips. Using a small ice cream scoop (or measure out 2 tablespoons per cookie), drop heaps of the mixture onto the greased cookie sheets, spacing them at least 1½ inches (4 cm) apart.
4. Bake for 12 to 15 minutes, until firm and just lightly browned. Immediately remove from the cookie sheet to a wire rack. Allow to cool completely before filling or storing in an airtight container.

COCONUT MACAROONS

Makes 16 cookies

2 egg whites
3 cups (300 g) shredded dried coconut
1½ teaspoons pure almond extract (see tip)
Pinch of salt
⅔ cup (200 g) sweetened condensed milk
Few drops of red food coloring (optional)
Confectioners' sugar, if needed

1. Preheat the oven to 350°F (180°C). Line a couple of cookie sheets with parchment paper.
2. In a small bowl, whip the egg whites with an electric mixer until stiff. Set aside.
3. Put the coconut, almond extract, salt, sweetened condensed milk, and food coloring in a medium bowl and stir until combined. Fold in the whipped egg whites until combined. Using a medium-size ice cream scoop (about 3 table-spoons), take scoopfuls of the mixture, packing it tightly by pressing against the side of the bowl or with another spoon. Drop flat side down onto the parchment-lined sheets, spacing them about 2 inches (5 cm) apart.
4. Use the palm of your hand or the bottom of a glass dipped in confectioners' sugar to gently flatten each scoop into a round about ½ inch (1 cm) high. The maca-roons will spread very little in the oven.
5. Bake for 8 minutes. Remove from the oven and leave on the cookie sheet for at least 5 minutes before transferring to a wire rack. Let cool completely before filling or storing in an airtight container.

TIP: For a milder flavor, substitute pure vanilla extract for the almond. The macaroons will come out a golden cream shade.

BEVERLY HILLS COOKIES

Makes 18 cookies

½ cup (115 g) butter, at room temperature

½ cup (110 g) firmly packed light brown sugar

½ cup (100 g) granulated white sugar

1 extra-large egg

½ teaspoon pure vanilla extract

1 cup (140 g) all-purpose flour, plus extra for flattening the cookies

1½ cups (110 g) old-fashioned rolled oats, whizzed to a fine powder in a blender or food
   processor (1¼ cups after blending)

½ teaspoon baking powder

½ teaspoon baking soda

¼ teaspoon salt

1 cup (170 g) semisweet chocolate chips

3 ounces (85 g) semisweet chocolate, grated

¾ cup (90 g) walnuts, toasted and chopped (optional)

1. Preheat the oven to 375°F (190°C).
2. With an electric mixer, beat together the butter and both sugars until creamy. Beat in the egg and vanilla extract until light and fluffy.
3. In a separate bowl, whisk together the flour, oat powder, baking powder, baking soda, and salt. Gradually add to the creamed mixture while stirring. Stir in the chocolate chips, grated chocolates, and walnuts.
4. Roll the dough into balls about 1½ inches (4 cm) in diameter. Place them 2 inches (5 cm) apart on an ungreased cookie sheet. Use the bottom of a glass to flatten to about 3 inches (7.5 cm) in diameter. To prevent sticking, dip the glass in flour before pressing each cookie.
5. Bake for 8 to 9 minutes, until the tops are firm. Immediately remove from the cookie sheet to a wire rack. Allow to cool completely before filling or storing in an airtight container.

AMARETTO BISCUITS

Makes 16 biscuits

1 cup (250 g) marzipan or almond paste
1 cup (200 g) superfine sugar
2 to 3 extra-large egg whites
¼ teaspoon pure almond extract
2 or 3 drops of red food coloring (optional)

1. Preheat the oven to 325°F (165°C). Line a cookie sheet with parchment paper.
2. Cut up the marzipan into small bits and put it in a medium bowl. Gradually knead in the sugar. Gradually knead in the egg whites (you may need more or less, depending on the consistency; shoot for very moist without being runny), almond extract, and food coloring, until the mixture is uniform and smooth.
3. Spoon out or use a pastry bag to pipe even amounts—about 1 teaspoonful for each biscuit—onto the lined cookie sheet, allowing a full 2 inches (5 cm) between the mounds. These really spread!
4. Bake for 20 to 25 minutes, until lightly golden and crispy around the edges. Remove and allow to cool before removing from the cookie sheet. If the paper sticks, lightly moisten the back of it with a damp tea towel, wait a minute, and then peel away. Use as required or store in an airtight container.

TIN ROOF COOKIES

Makes 12 cookies

4 tablespoons (60 g) butter, at room temperature, plus extra for greasing
½ cup (110 g) firmly packed light brown sugar
¼ cup (50 g) granulated white sugar
1 extra-large egg
½ cup (130 g) peanut butter, preferably chunky
¼ teaspoon baking soda
¼ teaspoon salt
½ teaspoon pure vanilla extract
1 to 1¼ cups (140 to 175 g) all-purpose flour
½ cup (85 g) semisweet chocolate chips

1. Preheat the oven to 375°F (190°C). Grease a couple of cookie sheets.
2. With an electric mixer, beat together the butter and both sugars until creamy. Beat in the egg, peanut butter, baking soda, salt, and vanilla extract until well combined.
3. Add the flour to the creamed mixture and blend well. Use the greater amount of flour if your peanut butter is especially oily. Stir in the chocolate chips.
4. Using a small ice cream scoop (or measuring out 2 tablespoons per cookie), drop heaps of dough about 3 inches (7.5 cm) apart onto the greased cookie sheets. Use the bottom of a glass to flatten the cookies.
5. Bake for 10 to 12 minutes, until golden and the edges are lightly browned. Immediately remove to a wire rack and cool completely. Use as required or store in an airtight container.

FRUITCAKE COOKIES

Makes 48 mini cookies

4 tablespoons (60 g) butter, at room temperature
¼ cup (55 g) firmly packed light brown sugar
¼ teaspoon baking soda
½ teaspoon ground cinnamon
⅛ teaspoon salt (about 3 pinches)
1 extra-large egg
½ teaspoon pure vanilla extract
½ cup plus 2 tablespoons (90 g) all-purpose flour
1 cup (125 g) pitted dates, coarsely chopped
½ cup (125 g) quartered candied cherries
½ cup (100 g) diced candied pineapple
¼ cup (30 g) walnuts, toasted and chopped
¼ cup (30 g) pecans, toasted and chopped
¼ cup (35 g) hazelnuts, toasted and chopped

1. Preheat the oven to 350°F (180°C). Either line the cups in mini cupcake pans with 48 paper liners or arrange 48 foil-lined paper cups for petit fours on a cookie sheet.
2. In a medium bowl, use an electric mixer to beat together the butter, sugar, baking soda, cinnamon, and salt until blended. Add the egg and vanilla extract and beat until fluffy.
3. In a separate bowl, mix the flour with the dates, cherries, and pineapple until the fruits are coated. Stir this mixture and the nuts into the butter mixture until blended. Drop small spoonfuls of the batter into the liners or cups, filling them only half full.
4. Bake for 11 to 13 minutes, until the tops look dry and the edges are beginning to brown. Leave in the pan on a wire rack until completely cool, then use as required or store in an airtight container.

MOCHA COOKIES

Makes 12 cookies

½ cup (115 g) butter, at room temperature, plus extra for greasing
½ cup (100 g) granulated white sugar
¼ cup (55 g) firmly packed light brown sugar
1 teaspoon pure vanilla extract
1 tablespoon instant espresso powder
1 extra-large egg
¾ cup plus 2 tablespoons (125 g) all-purpose flour
6 tablespoons (40 g) cocoa powder
¼ teaspoon salt
Scant ⅔ cup (100 g) milk chocolate chips
¼ cup (30 g) chopped toasted pecans

1. Preheat the oven to 350°F (180°C). Grease a cookie sheet.
2. Using an electric mixer with the beaters or paddle, beat together the butter, both sugars, vanilla extract, and espresso powder until incorporated. Scrape down the sides of the bowl with a rubber spatula, then beat on high speed for about 3 minutes, until fluffy.
3. Add the egg and beat well, scraping down the sides of the bowl as needed. Add the flour, cocoa, and salt and beat until blended. Add the chocolate chips and nuts and mix until incorporated.
4. Using a small ice cream scoop (or measuring out 2 tablespoons per cookie), drop heaps of the mixture onto the greased cookie sheet, forming 12 mounds about 1¼ inches (3 cm) apart.
5. Bake for 10 minutes, until the cookies appear set. Their centers should remain chewy and soft, so do not overcook. Once removed from the oven, allow the cookies to remain on the sheet for 1 minute before removing to a wire rack to cool completely. Once cool, use as required or store in an airtight container.

ZESTY MADELEINES

Makes 16 madeleines

5 tablespoons (75 g) butter, at room temperature, plus extra for greasing
½ cup (100 g) granulated white sugar
3 extra-large eggs
¾ cup (110 g) all-purpose flour
½ teaspoon baking powder
1 teaspoon finely grated orange zest

1. Preheat the oven to 400°F (200°C). Lightly grease 2 madeleine molds. You will need 16 shell-shaped cups total.
2. In a medium bowl, cream the butter with an electric mixer. Add the sugar and mix well. Add the eggs one at a time, beating well after each.
3. In a separate small bowl, whisk together the flour and baking powder. Stir in the orange zest until well coated.
4. Add the flour mixture to the butter mixture and incorporate well. Spoon the mixture into the molds and place the molds on cookie sheets.
5. Bake for 10 to 12 minutes, until lightly golden and the tops spring back when lightly pressed. Remove from the oven and immediately transfer the madeleines from the molds to a cooling rack. Cool completely before cutting and filling or storing in an airtight container.

BANANA BREAD

A version of this recipe was first introduced to me by a roomate in college, where it saw me through a number of late study nights. I've since introduced it to friends and colleagues in Mexico, France, and the United Kingdom. My family especially loves the bread for breakfast as a delicious alternative to their usual cereals. If used to make ice cream sandwiches, enjoy the sandwiches on the spot so that the bread remains firm.

Makes 1 standard loaf (8 servings) or 6 mini loaves

3 large or 4 medium very ripe bananas
½ cup (115 g) butter, at room temperature, plus extra for greasing
1 cup (200 g) granulated white sugar
2 extra-large eggs
2 cups (280 g) all-purpose flour, plus extra for the pans
2 teaspoons baking soda
¼ cup (30 g) walnuts, chopped

1. Preheat the oven to 350°F (180°C). Grease and flour an 8½ by 4½ by 2½-inch (22 by 11 by 6 cm) loaf pan or six mini loaf pans.
2. In a large bowl, vigorously mix the bananas until light and fluffy. In a medium bowl, cream the butter and sugar with an electric mixer. Cream them some more! Then add the eggs, one at a time, beating well after each addition.
3. Add the flour and baking soda and mix well. Add the bananas and stir until combined. Pour into the prepared loaf pan(s). Scatter the nuts on top.
4. Bake for 50 to 55 minutes if using a standard loaf pan or 25 to 30 minutes if using mini pans, until a cake tester inserted into the center comes out clean. Remove from the oven and cool in the pan(s) on a wire rack for 10 minutes before removing and allowing to cool fully. Use as required or store in an airtight container.

   TIP: If you've ever inadvertently bitten into a mouthful of baking soda, you will know that it tends to clump. Ensure your container is fully sealed, then give it a vigorous shake before opening to measure.

MOCHA LOAF

Makes 1 standard loaf; 10 servings

1 tablespoon instant coffee powder
¼ cup (60 ml) boiling water
1¼ cups (175 g) all-purpose flour, plus extra for the pan
¼ teaspoon salt
1½ teaspoons baking powder
½ cup (115 g) butter, at room temperature, plus extra for greasing
¾ cup (150 g) granulated white sugar
2 extra-large eggs
¼ cup (60 ml) milk
½ teaspoon pure vanilla extract
Scant ⅔ cup (100 g) semisweet chocolate chips

1. Preheat the oven to 350°F (180°C). Grease and flour an 8½ by 4½ by 2½-inch (22 by 11 by 6 cm) loaf pan.
2. Add the coffee powder to the boiling water and stir until dissolved. Let cool. In a medium bowl, whisk together the flour, salt, and baking powder and set aside.
3. With an electric mixer in a large bowl, beat the butter and sugar until creamy. Add the eggs, one at a time, beating well after each addition. Add one-third of the flour mixture, mixing on low speed just until combined. Add half the milk, half the coffee, and all of the vanilla extract, mixing until combined. Repeat with the flour, milk, and coffee, ending with the last third of the flour mixture. Stir in the chocolate chips and pour the batter into the prepared loaf pan.
4. Bake for 50 to 55 minutes, until a cake tester inserted in the center comes out clean. Cool in the pan on a wire rack for 10 minutes before removing and allowing to cool fully. Use as required or store in an airtight container.

CHOCOLATE CUPCAKES

I've included my recipe for chocolate cupcakes, which are used in my Cupcake Sundae (page 121) and cupshake recipes (pages 119 and 120). While this recipe makes a full dozen, you can always ice the extra ones or freeze for a later time.

Makes 12 cupcakes

3 ounces (85 g) unsweetened baking chocolate, 90 percent cacao
1 cup plus 2 tablespoons (160 g) all-purpose flour
¼ teaspoon baking soda
¼ teaspoon baking powder
¼ teaspoon salt
½ cup (115 g) butter, at room temperature
½ cup (100 g) granulated white sugar
½ cup (110 g) firmly packed light brown sugar
1 extra-large egg
½ cup (120 ml) buttermilk, at room temperature
1 teaspoon pure vanilla extract

1. Preheat the oven to 350°F (180°C). Line a 12-hole cupcake pan with paper liners (ideally waxed paper).
2. In a heatproof bowl, melt the chocolate in the microwave at 80 percent power for 1 minute, then stir. If needed, return to the microwave for 10 seconds at a time, stirring after each interval until smooth. Alternatively, you can put the heatproof bowl over a pan of hot (not boiling) water and stir until melted and smooth. Set aside to cool.
3. Whisk or sift the flour with the baking soda, baking powder, and salt. Set aside. In a medium bowl using an electric mixer, cream together the butter and both sugars. Add the egg and mix until incorporated, scraping down the sides of the bowl as needed. Pour in the cooled chocolate and mix. In a measuring cup, mix the buttermilk and vanilla extract.
4. Add the flour mixture in three additions and the buttermilk mixture in two additions, starting and ending with the flour. Mix just until incorporated after each addition; do not overmix or the cupcakes will be tough! Divide the batter evenly among the liners, filling each about two-thirds full.
5. Bake for 20 to 25 minutes, rotating the tray back to front halfway through, until a cake tester inserted into the center of a cupcake comes out clean. Allow to cool completely before adding to a cupshake or topping with ice cream.

THE ICE CREAM RECIPES

Nothing beats homemade when it comes to ice cream! When freshly prepared, the flavors really come alive. In this section, I've provided the recipes for the ice cream flavors most commonly used throughout this book. Whether you're hankering for something universal, such as vanilla or chocolate, or a lighter option, like lemon or marmalade, you'll find it here. Any of the recipes can be easily prepared on its own or combined with a cookie option of your choosing.

VANILLA ICE CREAM

Makes 1½ to 2 pints (700 to 950 ml)

2 cups (480 ml) heavy or whipping cream
Pinch of salt
6 tablespoons (75 g) granulated white sugar
¼ vanilla bean
1 teaspoon pure vanilla extract

1. Scald ½ cup (120 ml) of the cream over low heat (but do not boil). Add the salt and sugar and stir until dissolved.
2. Remove from the heat, add the vanilla bean, and allow to soak for at least 5 minutes. Then split the vanilla bean, split lengthwise, scrape the seeds into the cream mixture, and discard the pod.
3. Pour into a heatproof bowl, allow to come to room temperature, then chill in the refrigerator.
4. Once cool, stir in the vanilla extract and the remaining 1½ cups (360 ml) of cream. Pour into an ice cream maker and follow the manufacturer's instructions. When finished churning, transfer to an airtight plastic container, allowing at least ½ inch (1 cm) of empty space at the top of the container, as the mixture will expand as it freezes. Allow to freeze for at least 2 hours.

CHOCOLATE ICE CREAM

Makes about 1½ pints (700 ml)

1 cup (170 g) semisweet chocolate chips
1 cup (240 ml) heavy or whipping cream
3 extra-large egg yolks
¼ teaspoon salt

1. In a small heatproof bowl, melt the chocolate chips in the microwave on 80 percent power for 1 minute. Stir and heat again for 10 seconds, then stir and repeat in 10-second intervals until smooth. Alternatively, put the heatproof bowl over a pan of hot (not boiling) water and stir until melted.
2. Transfer to a medium bowl and set aside for 10 minutes (but no longer).
3. Meanwhile, in a separate medium bowl, whip the cream until stiff and set aside.
4. Add the egg yolks and salt to the cooled chocolate and stir with a whisk just until combined. Fold into the whipped cream mixture.
5. Spoon into an airtight plastic container, allowing at least ½ inch (1 cm) of empty space at the top of the container, as the mixture will expand as it freezes. Allow to freeze for at least 1½ hours.

MOCHA ICE CREAM

Makes about 1½ pints (700 ml)

2 teaspoons instant coffee granules
1 teaspoon boiling water
½ cup (85 g) milk chocolate chips
¾ cup (180 ml) heavy cream
2 extra-large egg whites

1. In a heatproof cup, dissolve the coffee granules in the boiling water. Then combine the coffee, chocolate chips, and ¼ cup (60 ml) of the cream in a small heatproof bowl.

2. Microwave on 80 percent power for 1 minute, then stir well to help the chips melt. Return to the microwave and repeat for 10-second intervals, stirring well each time until the mixture is smooth. Alternatively, put the heatproof bowl over a pan of hot (not boiling) water and stir until the mixture is melted and smooth. Transfer to a larger bowl to cool for 10 to 15 minutes.

3. In a small, clean bowl, whisk the egg whites until stiff peaks form. Fold into the cooled chocolate mixture. In another small bowl, beat the remaining ½ cup (120 ml) of cream until stiff peaks form; also fold this into the chocolate mixture.

4. Spoon into an airtight plastic container, allowing at least ½ inch (1 cm) of empty space at the top of the container, as the mixture will expand as it freezes. Allow to freeze for at least 1½ hours.

MASCARPONE ICE CREAM

Makes 1½ to 2 pints (700 to 950 ml)

2 extra-large egg yolks
1 teaspoon cornstarch
⅓ cup plus 1 tablespoon (80 g) superfine sugar
5 tablespoons (75 ml) whole milk
¼ teaspoon ground nutmeg
1 cup (250 g) mascarpone cheese
⅔ cup (200 g) *fromage frais* or low-fat cream cheese

1. In a medium bowl with an electric mixer, whisk together the yolks, cornstarch, and sugar until light and fluffy. Bring the milk and nutmeg to a gentle simmer in a small saucepan over low heat

2. Remove the warmed milk from the heat and whisk little by little into the egg mixture. Then return the entire mixture to the saucepan and bring back to a gentle simmer, whisking continuously. Do not allow to clump.

3. Remove from the heat. Pour into a heatproof bowl, cover, and cool to room temperature, then chill in the refrigerator.

4. Once chilled, pour into an ice cream maker, along with the mascarpone and *fromage frais*, and follow the manufacturer's instructions. Transfer to an airtight plastic container, allowing at least ½ inch (1 cm) of empty space at the top of the container, as the mixture will expand as it freezes. Allow to freeze for at least 2 hours.

MARMALADE ICE CREAM

Makes about 1 pint (480 ml)

½ cup (160 g) orange marmalade
½ cup (120 ml) evaporated milk
1 tablespoon granulated white sugar
1 teaspoon cornstarch
½ cup plus 1 tablespoon (140 ml) heavy
    cream, chilled

1. In a small microwave-proof bowl, heat the marmalade in the microwave on 80 percent power for 30 seconds. Stir vigorously to break up the lumps. Repeat for another 30 seconds and stir until smooth. Alternatively, put in a heatproof bowl over a pan of hot (not boiling) water and stir vigorously to break up the lumps. Once smooth, remove from the heat.

2. Pour the evaporated milk into a small saucepan. Add the cornstarch and whisk until combined. Add the sugar and heat to thicken the mixture, stirring constantly, just until small bubbles begin to form. Remove from the heat just before it starts to boil. Let cool.

3. Using an electric mixer, whip the cream until soft peaks form. Pour in half of the cooled milk mixture and fold into the whipped cream. Repeat with the remaining half. Once the marmalade has cooled to room temperature, fold in until well incorporated.

4. If using to fill ice cream sandwiches, you can spread onto the cookies before freezing. Otherwise, spoon into an airtight plastic container, allowing at least ½ inch (1 cm) of empty space at the top of the container, as the mixture will expand as it freezes. Allow to freeze for at least 1 hour.

LEMON ICE CREAM

Makes about 1½ pints (700 ml)

1½ cups (360 ml) whipping cream
½ cup plus 1 tablespoon granulated
    white sugar (115 g)
¼ cup (60 ml) fresh lemon juice (about
    1½ to 2 lemons)
5 teaspoons finely grated lemon zest (about
    2 lemons)

1. Put the cream, sugar, lemon juice, and zest in a medium (but deep) bowl. Using an electric mixer with the beaters or paddle, beat until completely combined and slightly thickened. Be sure to scrape any zest off the beaters and stir it back into the cream mixture with a spoon or spatula before freezing.

2. Pour into an airtight plastic storage container. Allow at least ½ inch (1 cm) of empty space at the top of the container, as the mixture will expand as it freezes. Freeze for at least 2 hours.

REFRESHING TREATS

At Buttercup Cake Shop, we've found a number of good uses for our ice cream beyond sandwiches. Sometimes our customers want a filling treat that will also quench their thirst. For these occasions, we recommend a cupshake (pages 119 and 120)—your favorite cupcake blended with vanilla ice cream and milk into a really thick milkshake. Or when customers want a lighter refreshment, a Cola Float (page 122) usually fits the bill. And for those who want to enjoy their cake and ice cream with a spoon, we offer a Cupcake Sundae (page 121). In this section you'll find recommendations for how to get the best results for each of these treats.

COOKIES 'N' CREAM CUPSHAKE

Whoever first put together vanilla ice cream and Oreo cookies was a genius! I think we've gone one step better at Buttercup by combining vanilla ice cream with our cookies 'n' cream cupcake, and now this is our top-selling cupshake flavor. If you are short on time, you can skip making the buttercream in the first step and simply add 2 Oreo cookies and 2 tablespoons whipped cream straight into the blender with the other ingredients.

Makes 1 large cupshake

1 teaspoon (5 g) butter, at room temperature
2 tablespoons confectioners' sugar
2 tablespoons whipped cream
2 Oreo cookies, crushed
2 large scoops softened vanilla ice cream, homemade (page 112) or store-bought
1 chocolate cupcake, homemade (page 109) or store-bought
½ cup (125 ml) cold whole or part-skim milk, plus more if required

1. In a small bowl using a mini whisk, mix the butter and confectioners' sugar until smooth. Fold in the whipped cream and crushed cookies, then set aside.
2. Ensure the ice cream is taken out of the freezer far enough in advance to soften to scooping texture. Put 2 large, rounded scoops in a blender. The scoopfuls should be well packed without pockets of air or you will end up with a cupshake that is too liquid.
3. Cut the cupcake into quarters, discard the paper liner, and add to the blender. Use a large spoon to push down the cake as much as possible. This step is necessary to ensure the cake grinds up rather than remaining in chunks. Pour the cold milk over the cupcake. Add the Oreo mixture.
4. Place the top securely on the blender and blend on low speed for 20 seconds. Switch to high speed until a normal milkshake consistency is achieved. Turn off the blender and use a spoon to make sure any chunks of cake at the bottom have broken up.
5. If you find the milkshake is too thick to mix properly, you can add up to 2 tablespoons more milk. Do not add more than this or it will be too liquid.
6. Pour into a serving cup, filling to within ⅛ inch (3 mm) of the rim. Serve immediately with a wide straw and long spoon. (The mixture will be too thick to enjoy through a narrow straw!)

CHOCOLATE CUPSHAKE

When you're hungry but also wanting refreshment, this cupshake will fit the bill. A combination of milkshake and cupcake, the blend is truly decadent! At Buttercup, our cupcakes are always thickly iced with chocolate buttercream. Avoid fondant, however, as it doesn't blend well. For a simpler treat, use a cupcake without icing.

Makes 1 large cupshake

2 large scoops softened vanilla ice cream, homemade (page 112) or store-bought
1 chocolate cupcake, homemade (page 109) or store-bought
½ cup (125 ml) cold whole or part-skim milk, plus more if required

1. Ensure the ice cream is taken out of the freezer far enough in advance to soften to scooping texture. Put 2 large, rounded scoops in a blender. The scoopfuls should be well packed without pockets of air or you will end up with a cupshake that is too liquid.
2. Remove any fondant or nonedible decoration from your cupcake. Cut it into quarters, discard the paper liner, and add to the blender. With a large spoon, push down the cake as much as possible. This step is necessary to ensure the cake grinds up rather than remaining in chunks. Pour the cold milk over the cupcake.
3. Place the top securely on the blender and blend on low speed for 20 seconds. Switch to high speed until a normal milkshake consistency is achieved. Turn off the blender and use a spoon to make sure any chunks of cake at the bottom have broken up.
4. If you find that the milkshake is too thick to mix properly, you can add up to 2 tablespoons more milk. Do not add more than this or it will be too liquid.
5. Pour into a serving cup, filling to within ⅛ inch (3 mm) of the rim. Serve immediately with a wide straw and a long spoon. (The mixture will be too thick to enjoy through a narrow straw!)

CUPCAKE SUNDAE

This treat will take you back to childhood birthday parties, as it combines the favorites of cake and ice cream, plus the added indulgence of an easy homemade chocolate sauce!

Makes 1 sundae

¼ cup (55 g) semisweet chocolate chips
2 tablespoons plus 2 teaspoons whipping cream
1 chocolate cupcake, homemade (page 109) or store-bought
2 large scoops softened vanilla ice cream, homemade (page 112) or store-bought
1 tablespoon chocolate sprinkles and/or flakes (optional)

1. To prepare the chocolate sauce, combine the chocolate chips and cream in a small microwave-proof bowl and microwave on high power for 10 to 20 seconds, until the cream is hot and the chocolate starts to melt. Stir until the chocolate is completely melted and the mixture is thick and smooth. If necessary, return to the microwave for another 10 seconds, until melted. Stir well until no lumps remain. Alternatively, you can put the mixture in a small heatproof bowl over a pan of hot (not boiling) water and stir constantly until completely melted.

2. Set the mixture aside and allow to thicken slightly. (If it becomes too stiff to serve, you can reheat for a couple of seconds in the microwave or over the pan of hot water.) Remove the paper liner from the cupcake and put the cupcake upright in a sundae glass or small serving bowl.

3. Fit a pastry bag with a toothed icing nozzle and fold over the top of the bag around your cupped hand. Fill with the ice cream. Working quickly, push the ice cream down toward the nozzle, pressing out any air bubbles.

4. Gently pipe the ice cream around the edge of the cupcake, then work your way in a spiral toward the center. The ice cream should completely cover the cupcake. End with a flourish in the center as you pull away the nozzle.

5. With a spoon, drizzle the chocolate sauce over the ice cream. Add sprinkles or flakes and serve immediately with a sturdy spoon.

COLA FLOAT

On the one hand it seems a bit silly, really, to include a "recipe" for a cola float especially as it has only two ingredients. But the younger generation tends to be unfamiliar with cola floats, so we get asked about them a lot at the shops. A treat that was particularly beloved in American malt shops in the 1950s, cola floats have proven to be very popular today with all ages. We prefer regular cola; however, diet cola can be substituted and still makes a delicious treat!

Makes 1 large cola float

1 large scoop plus 1 tablespoon vanilla ice cream, homemade (page 112) or store-bought
1½ cups (360 ml) cola, very cold

1. Place the scoop of ice cream in a tall glass, then add the single tablespoonful. The tablespoonful will float separately to the top when served, so that you can enjoy the wonderful combination of creamy ice cream and effervescent cola right from the first mouthful!
2. Tip the glass 45 degrees, then very, *very* slowly pour in the cola, aiming to hit just below the rim so as to control the amount of foam. The key to success is in slow and careful pouring, so take your time.
3. When the foam reaches the top of the glass, pause if necessary before topping up with cola. You should be able to get all or most of it into a large glass. Serve with either a straw-spoon or a separate tall straw and long spoon.

TIP: Other people swear by the method of putting the cola in the glass first, then adding the ice cream. I call this method the "cannon bomb," because it can lead to uncontrolled foaming and overflowing. So although it is definitely quicker, adopt it at your own risk!

INDEX

ABOUT THE AUTHOR

Donna Egan founded the Buttercup Cake Shop, London's first cupcakery, in 2006. Its original location in London's Kensington was soon joined by two outlets: in Westfield London and Kent. In 2011, Buttercup opened its fourth outlet on the site of the 2012 Olympics in the new Westfield Stratford City, the largest shopping center in Europe. Buttercup has been recognized in many publications, including *Time Out*, *Metro*, *Daily Mail*, *Financial Times*, Condé Nast's *Brides*, and *British Baker*.

Buttercup began selling ice cream sandwiches and cupshakes in spring 2011. They proved instantly popular with customers of all ages and became the impetus for writing this book.

Donna combines a corporate background in consumer marketing with her role as a "mum who bakes." Originally from California, she has lived in London for twelve years and previously lived and worked in Mexico and France. Today she lives in South London with her husband and two daughters, aged fourteen and nine, who also love to bake.